Professional Tips and Techniques Series

Detailing Cars & Trucks

A mini-course for the do-it-yourselfer who wants to learn how to do it right.

Do-It-Right Publishing, Inc.

Published and distributed by

Do-It-Right Publishing, Inc.
147 East Holly Street, Suite 304
Pasadena, CA 91103

Written by:	Dennis Holmes
	Michael Bishop
Series concept and design by:	Dennis Holmes
Production by:	Steve Janowski
Photography by:	Michael Bishop
	Patrick Holmes
Illustration by:	Steve Amos

FIRST EDITION
Third printing

Library of Congress Card Number: 91-71748

ISBN 1-879110-17-2

Proudly Printed in the United States of America

FOREWORD

This book addresses one of the most important areas of modern service: total vehicle appearance care. Or, as it is commonly called: *detailing*. The DIY jobs taught in this book require absolutely no mechanical skill, yet they are some of the biggest money savers. For example, do your own complete exterior-and-interior detail job, and you will save $100-200!

Good detailing has two other important benefits besides saving money: (1) you get the immediate reward of a much nicer looking "ride," and (2) you will find a pot of gold at the end of the rainbow when the time comes to sell your car or truck.

Both car dealers and private buyers regard appearance as an extremely important factor in assessing value. You can expect from $500 to $5000 more at resale time from a well-detailed sharp-looking vehicle instead of one that's "showing its age." (Actually more for exotics and collectible cars.)

Our approach is *practical.* We teach you how to do show-quality detailing, for the ultimate level of quality. We also address the "ordinary" needs for a quick wash and wax job on your daily driver. We tested a number of quick-wash methods to come up with what we show you here. And we know that one-step cleaner-polish products do an excellent job, so we show you how to use them properly.

Our method of instruction is simple: you will learn by looking. This book has almost 400 photos showing you how to do each task, step-by-step. (Our cover says "Over 340 photos," but it went to print before we had completed our final count!) The cars and trucks you see in our projects are not exotics—they are typical of the cars and trucks most of you are driving. They present real-world detailing problems, and you will find it easy to translate what you learn here to your own vehicle.

Some of the most important "tools" of detailing are cleaning and polishing products. We have included photos of a number of the products that we purchased and used in writing this book. The ones we show worked well for us. But do not construe the absence of any product as a lack of endorsement. We simply ran out of space in our shopping cart! This is not a product *comparison* book, it is a product *understanding* book.

As with other books in the Do-It-Right *Professional Tips and Techniques Series,* this book gives you a mini-course in an important area of automotive DIY work. It's goal is to build life-long skills that will enable you to produce top-quality results. And while the book is designed so that each section stands alone, we encourage you to read it cover-to-cover for a rich understanding of the subject. We want you to know not only *what* the professionals do, but *why.*

THANKS

Thanks to our partners—Steve McKee, Lonetta Holmes, and John Dawson. They gave us the enthusiastic encouragement we needed to launch this new series of books.

Thanks to John Herrmann, Alex Litrov, Robert Beck, and Viola Pitcher for their technical assistance with detailing products.

Thanks to Jana Brett for her assistance in cover design. Thanks to Dan Hackett and Karl Anthony for their technical assistance with Ventura Publisher.

Thanks to Nissan Motor Corporation in U.S.A. and Hyundai Motor America for their support and endorsement of our model-specific series of manuals. They have helped validate our highly visual approach to this type of book, and they have made a lot of their customers quite happy in the process.

And thanks to the 35,000+ professional technicians and vehicle-preparation experts in Toyota, Nissan, Honda, and Hyundai dealerships for whom we have developed factory training programs and manuals over the past 18 years. It was *you* who taught, and we who learned.

IMPORTANT SAFETY NOTICE

Pay special heed to the *warnings* in this book. They are intended to help protect you and your vehicle. When lifting your vehicle, make sure it is securely supported on jackstands before performing any work underneath it. Do *not* rely on the jack that came with your car or truck for safe support.

You should use standard and accepted safety precautions and equipment when handling toxic or flammable fluids. You should wear safety goggles or other protection during cutting, grinding, chiseling, prying, or any other similar process that can cause material removal or projectiles.

Following proper service procedures is essential for your safety and the correct functioning of your vehicle. We believe that the general service procedures in this book are described in such a manner that they may be performed safely and properly on a wide variety of vehicles. However, it is your responsibility to determine the precise applicability of these procedures to your specific vehicle or engine.

Please note that the condition of your vehicle, or the level of your mechanical skill, or your level of reading comprehension may result in or contribute in some way to an occurrence which causes injury to yourself or damage to your vehicle. It is not possible to anticipate all of the conceivable ways or conditions under which cars and trucks may be serviced, or to provide warnings as to all of the possible hazards that may result. Accordingly, because of these conditions which are unknown to us and are beyond our control, our liability must be and is limited to the cost of this book.

If you use service procedures, tools, or parts which are not specifically recommended in this book you must first completely satisfy yourself that neither your safety nor the safety of your vehicle will be jeopardized. All liability is expressly disclaimed for any injury or damage if you fail in any respect to follow all of the instructions and warnings given in any procedure in this book.

Although the information in this book is based on industry sources and experts, it is possible that changes in designs may be made which could not be included here. While striving for precise accuracy, Do-It-Right Publishing, Inc. cannot assume responsibility for any errors, changes, or omissions that may occur in the information presented here.

Contents At-a-Glance

Detailed Contents

Section 1:

The Detailing Process

WHAT IS DETAILING?

Detailing is the process of cleaning and preserving an automobile—with careful attention to *detail.* Quality detailing can bring out the very best appearance of your car or truck and give you instant enjoyment. If you detail your vehicle *regularly,* you can expect it to last longer and bring a higher price at resale time. Detailing involves (1) analyzing the type of paint, trim, wheels, and upholstery, (2) selecting the correct products and tools for each surface, and (3) using the proper techniques to get professional results. In this section, we give you a fast visual overview of the steps in the detailing process, as shown on a number of our project vehicles. This is *what* you need to do to produce fine results. The rest of this book shows you *how.*

EXTERIOR CLEANING

Wash entire vehicle.
Proper detailing always begins with a thorough washing. Spray-on/rinse-off chemical cleaners can be a big help on wheels. And a proper brush is essential for tires and soft tops.

Clean oxidation from paint. Frequent waxing slows oxidation—it does not eliminate it. In the past, cleaners usually contained an abrasive, but modern clear-coat finishes will not tolerate abrasives. Section 2 explains the different products available, and Section 5 shows you typical cleaning jobs on a number of vehicles.

Clean oxidation and rust from trim. There is a wide variety of trim on today's cars and trucks: chrome-plated steel, chrome-plated plastic, plastic, aluminum, rubber, black painted trim, etc. Cleaning each requires correct products and techniques, as explained in Section 6.

Shampoo convertible top. *Since a convertible top is an important part of the "character" of such a car, it is critically important that it be perfectly spotless and clean. Section 7 shows you how.*

Deep clean wheels and wheel covers. *Brake dust is a problem on almost all front wheels. Chrome, wire, and painted steel wheels can rust. Aluminum wheels oxidize over time. Section 8 gives you important tips on cleaning every type of wheel. Be sure to use the right product for your type of wheels.*

Deep clean tires. *Special tire cleaners will help you remove not only road dirt but also the stubborn brown oxidation that discolors both blackwalls and whitewalls. A proper brush is essential.*

EXTERIOR POLISH, WAX, & PROTECT

Polish the paint.
Cleaners do a great job of restoring color and shine. But polish or "glaze" (1) buffs the surface to produce a more intense shine, and (2) fills in microscopic scratches.

Apply carnauba wax to paint and hard trim. *Wax protects the surface and retards oxidation. Wax also adds a final gloss— but not much! (The secret to a great shine is proper cleaning and polishing before you apply wax.) A critical part of a professional quality job is removing all dried wax residue from emblems, door handles, and body seams.*

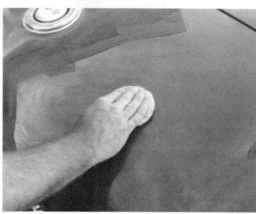

Apply protectant to all exterior vinyl and rubber. *The goal is to restore the color and sheen to tires, vinyl convertible and soft tops, and soft rubber and vinyl trim. The special applicator shown in Section 8 can eliminate overspray mess.*

Clean all windows and mirrors. *This is done as the last exterior step because a power buffer may "spray" some cleaner or polish onto the windows. We recommend a specialized alcohol-based cleaner and a lint-free cotton towel. Perfect cleaning of corners and edges is important.*

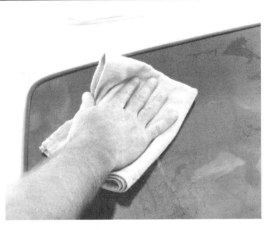

INTERIOR CLEANING & CONDITIONING

Vacuum, shampoo, and protect carpets. *Foam shampoo does a good job of cleaning without getting the carpet soaking wet. Finish with Scotchgard or similar treatment.*

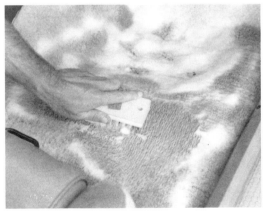

Vacuum, clean, and protect upholstery. *Fabric, leather, and vinyl each require appropriate products and techniques as discussed in Sections 2 and 9.*

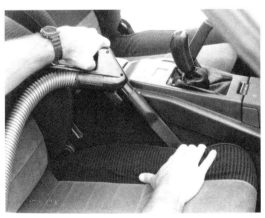

Clean and protect door panels, door sills, steering wheel, pedals, and headliner. *These are often overlooked, yet thorough cleaning and the correct protectant makes a big difference in appearance.*

Detail the dashboard. *This job takes some time—cleaning instrument faces, swabbing the inside of air-conditioning ducts, polishing chrome, cleaning the glovebox, etc. Yet this is the "face" of the vehicle to the driver, so it needs much more than just a simple dusting.*

Vacuum and clean the trunk. *Most pros peter out here, except for show cars. But it is a part of a perfect job, as described in Section 9.*

OPTIONAL UNDERHOOD & CHASSIS DETAILING

Wash engine and engine compartment. *If it's not too dirty, this can be done with a solvent product and a hose, as shown in Section 10.*

Engine detailing. *The job here is to clean and polish all chrome, aluminum, plastic, rubber, and painted surfaces. You use the same chemicals as on exterior surfaces. In addition, underhood detailing usually requires some spot painting, as shown in Section 10.*

Clean wheel wells and chassis. *If you've got a high-riding 4x4 truck, the running gear is a visible and important part of its cosmetic appearance, as shown in Section 11. For show cars, chassis detailing is essential. And Section 8 gives you a "taste" of what's required.*

DETAILING IN A HURRY?

Once you've got your car or truck in top shape from a total deep detailing job, keeping it up is not overly time-consuming. Nonetheless, in the spirit of recognizing that we do not all live to spend endless hours of prime weekend time on our cars and trucks, we offer Sections 12 and 13.

Section 12 shows you how to do a 15-minute quick wash. While not in the tradition of car buffs, it will still produce fine results, leave your wax intact, and get you on your way to more important things.

Section 13 shows you how to use a one-step cleaner-wax product. Many professionals in the detailing business sneer at this type of product. But the fact that they are best-sellers tells us that do-it-yourselfers want them. We give you some tips for great results.

Section 2:

Detailing Products

WHAT'S IN THE NAME?

Choosing the correct chemical products is critical for your success in detailing. They are the "tools" of the job. Yet there are no industry-standard *names* for these products! In the store you will find wax that is called "glaze," liquid compound that is called "polish," and so forth. You must also distinguish between single-purpose products, such as "cleaner" and "wax," and dual-purpose products, such as "cleaner-and-wax" (which is often called "polish"). This was pretty confusing to us too, so don't feel alone! In this section, we have included photos of many of the products available. We have grouped the products by *what they do.* We have not included every product available in the marketplace—just a sampling to put some "faces" with our terminology.

WASH PRODUCTS

Tar and bug remover: *A "solvent" that is applied before washing. It helps soften and remove road tar, bugs, tree sap, and bird droppings.*

Automotive wash soap: *For routine washing. These special products are very mild and do not remove wax. Dishwashing liquid detergent will strip off wax, and should not be used. TIP: If your vehicle is not very dirty, use just plain water and elbow grease!*

Wash mitts: *Highly recommended. They hold a lot of water and are very gentle on the finish. Mitts are critical to the success of both the 2-bucket wash (Section 4) and the 15-minute quick wash (Section 12). We prefer mitts over sponges because they are less likely to scratch the surface with embedded dirt.*

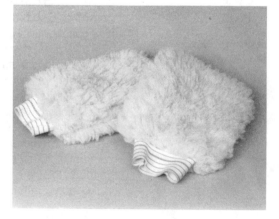

Chamois and towels: *A chamois is great for quickly getting a car "almost dry." But we like to use clean, dry terry-cloth towels to polish the finish and get rid of all final spots and streaks. Use "retired" bathroom towels or cheap industrial towels, which are available in bulk.*

PRO TIP: Choosing a Chamois

We found that we have a slight preference for a synthetic chamois over a natural skin. The synthetic type seems to be softer and does a better job of absorbing water. This is totally different than our memory of these synthetic products just a few years ago, so you might want to try one and see what you think. Different brands may vary in quality.

When buying a genuine leather chamois, make sure you understand the *size* you're getting. Some price leaders are almost too small to do the job. The good ones are not cheap, but they will last for years, if you treat them well.

When you're finished with a chamois, rinse it well in plain water, squeeze it out, and shake it to reshape it. Allow it to dry at room temperature. After its first use, a chamois will become quite hard when it dries. So when you're ready to use it again, soak it in a bucket of plain water or spray it with your hose. Wring it out, shake it, and you're back in the drying business!

PRO TIP: Understanding The Three Basic Jobs that Paint Products Do

No matter what type of wax you use, paint *will* oxidize and get dull over time. To restore the color and shine, there are three basic steps: (1) cleaning the paint to remove dirt and oxidation, (2) polishing the paint to produce maximum shine, and (3) applying wax to the paint to preserve the finish. We have classified detailing products in this section by these basic three functions. If you understand what your paint *needs,* you will be better able to select appropriate products.

Step 1. Paint cleaner or "deoxidizer" removes dirt and the dull outer skin of oxidation that forms on paint. These products come in a variety of strengths— from those with strong abrasives and chemicals to more gentle chemical cleaners that are safe for clear-coat paint.

Step 2. Polish or "glaze" restores shine, fills micro-scratches, and brings out the depth in the paint. Polish products usually contain a small amount of extremely fine abrasive and other "secret" chemicals to produce a shine. For a "wet-look," many pros use two grades: fine and ultrafine.

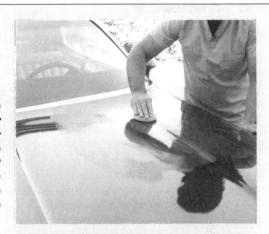

Step 3. Wax puts a protective coat over the paint. *The primary purpose of wax is to protect the paint, but it also adds depth and shine. After the wax dries, the residue is buffed off by hand.*

The end result of the three basic steps. *Notice the shine and depth on the driver's side of the hood, as compared to the untouched side.*

Every detailing job you do will include cleaning, polishing, and waxing the paint. Pros tend to use separate products for each step because of the control it provides and the excellent results it produces. (This is the process we teach in Section 5.) Many do-it-yourselfers find that a combination cleaner-polish followed by a pure wax is very satisfactory. And a huge number of people prefer the convenience of a one-step combination cleaner-polish-wax product, which we focus on in Section 13. So long as you *understand* these three steps—and see how some products combine them—you'll be better able to decipher labels and understand what you're buying.

PAINT CLEANER

Cleaners or "deoxidizers" for clear-coat paint: The labels on these products say "non-abrasive" or "safe for use on clear-coat paints." They also work just fine on conventional paint. They use chemicals and (in some) a small amount of ultrafine abrasive.

Cleaners or "deoxidizers" for non-clear-coat paint: These contain a fine abrasive to clean away oxidation more quickly. Use them on badly weathered conventional paint, but never on clear-coat. For lightly weathered conventional paint, we recommend you use a non-abrasive cleaner.

When selecting a cleaner, read the label carefully. These two bottles appear identical, yet the abrasive cleaner (on the left) is designed for vehicles with con ventional (non-clear-coat) paint. This type of choice is less obvious when you do not find the two types of product side by side!

ONE GRAND 'HEAVY DUTY CLEANER is for extremely oxidized finishes only. This product should be used only on paint that is a solid color or a 1 stage metallic where the finish is completely flat (no gloss) and very dry to the touch.

DO NOT USE THIS PRODUCT ON A NEW CLEAR COAT.

SHAKE WELL BEFORE USING

DIRECTIONS: ONE GRAND HEAVY DUTY CLEANER may be hand or machine applied.

Most heavy-duty cleaners will warn you not to use them on clear-coat. *Always read the label to be safe. Non-abrasive cleaners usually say "recommended for clear-coat."*

PAINT POLISH

"Polish" or "glaze" or "resealer." These names describe similar products. They usually contain fine polishing agents and fillers for microscopic scratches to produce more shine and depth in paint than cleaner alone can produce.

Ultrafine polish or glaze: *Only a few professional lines have such a product. These are intended for a second step after polishing to generate even more intensity and wet look in the paint. These products usually contain fillers for the microscopic swirl marks left from the buffing process, and are sometimes called "swirl remover."*

CARNAUBA WAX

Paste wax: *Carnauba-based wax (with no cleaner or polish) is preferred by professional and enthusiast detailers. Carnauba wax comes from a species of palm trees in Brazil, and is one of the hardest types of wax available.*

Liquid wax: *This particular product is called a "glaze," but it is in fact a premium wax— with no cleaner or polish. This again illustrates our advice to read the label to fully understand the purpose of a product. By the way, since the hard work is in cleaning and polishing, we have no preference in paste versus liquid wax.*

PRO TIP: Are Polymer Sealants Good for Your Paint?

Many sealants are made from polyurethane base with a hardener or polymer resin that puts a tough, clear "skin" on an automotive finish. This type of sealant can last up to 18 months. The problem is that some *cannot be removed!* They must wear off, yet oxidation of the paint underneath can continue, caused by ultraviolet rays. It is possible to end up with dull looking paint, and no way to get to the surface to clean and deoxidize it! Most of the professional detailers and industry experts we interviewed preferred conventional carnauba-type wax. We have found no reason to disagree with them.

ONE-STEP CLEANER-WAX

One-step cleaner-polish-wax: These products are time savers. The ones shown here are safe for clear-coat finishes, and specify that on the packaging. Although not intended for concours shows, they produce excellent results.

Many one-step products are available for either conventional or clear-coat paint. *Make sure you choose the product that matches your needs. The major difference is the amount of abrasive in the product.*

Read labels carefully. *This product is safe for clear-coat. It states "non-abrasive formula," and "safe for all modern finishes."*

PRO TIP: Is Teflon a Miracle Ingredient?

In *Professional Car Washing & Detailing* Magazine, an executive of DuPont (the makers of Teflon) was quoted as saying "The addition of a Teflon flouropolymer resin does nothing to enhance the properties of a car wax. We have no data that indicates the use of Teflon flouropolymer resins is beneficial in car waxes, and we have not seen data from other people that supports this position. Unless Teflon is applied at 700°F, it is not a viable ingredient, and it is useless in protecting the paint's finish." In discussing Teflon with professional detailers, we have yet to find any who recommend it.

COMPOUNDS

Polishing compound:
"Compound" means abrasive. Polishing compound is for cutting through heavy oxidation on conventional paint finishes. Never use it on clear-coat. Do not confuse this product with "polish," which is discussed on page 15.

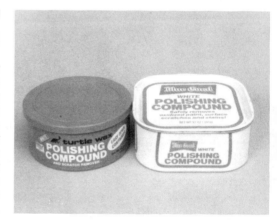

Rubbing compound:
These products contain an extremely strong abrasive for cutting through heavily weathered paint. They are much stronger than polishing compound, above. These can easily cut right through to bare metal, so be very careful!

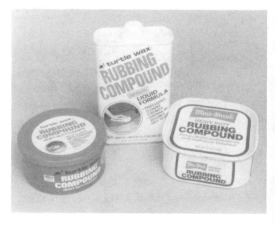

SPRAY-ON WHEEL CLEANERS

All-purpose wheel cleaner: *These products cut through brake dust and dirt, but are safe for all types of wheels. A good choice if you're not sure what type of wheel you have.*

Chrome and wire wheel cleaner: *A stronger product with chemicals and acid to cut rust. Use only on chrome-plated wheels, hub caps, and wire wheels. Do not use on plastic, aluminum, or painted surfaces. Follow the manufacturer's directions and warnings carefully. Some products are sold in a packaged kit with a neutralizer chemical.*

Aluminum and magnesium wheel cleaner: *Two types are available—a milder wash for anodized or polished aluminum and a stronger product with acid for rough-textured (as-cast) aluminum or magnesium wheels.*

UPHOLSTERY & CARPET PRODUCTS

Fabric and upholstery shampoo: An effective product for cleaning cloth or vinyl seats and door panels. We also use it on convertible tops.

Carpet cleaner and shampoo: The dry foam cleans carpeting effectively without getting it soaking wet. Some milder products also work well on fabric upholstery.

Leather cleaner and conditioner: These products are formulated for the needs of quality leather—to remove dirt and replenish oils that keep the leather supple. If you have vinyl-coated leather, the conditioner won't provide as much benefit, since it can't penetrate as well.

SPECIALIZED CLEANERS & PROTECTANTS

Tire cleaner: *For removing oxidation (the ugly brown color) on either blackwall or whitewall tires. "Whitewall" cleaning products work equally well on blackwalls.*

Exterior rubber and vinyl (ERV) protectant: *These popular products are used on tires, soft trim, vinyl roofs, interiors, soft bumpers, etc. They both clean and provide protection against deterioration from ozone in the air. Some pros prefer brands which produce less shine.*

Chrome and metal polish: *These versatile products usually contain both chemical and abrasive to cut through rust and oxidation. Use them on items like chrome wheels, bumpers, chrome metal trim, door handles, etc. Essential for proper detailing.*

Plastic polish: This is an ultrafine abrasive polish for use on the plastic parts that are so prevalent on modern cars. One of our big discoveries was how useful this polish is for such items as convertible windows, chrome-plated plastic trim, instrument faces, etc. Highly recommended.

Alcohol-based glass cleaner: This type of product cuts road grime and leaves glass clearer than the more common household ammonia types. Available at most automotive stores.

Engine cleaner: These products contain detergent and solvents to remove grease and grime from the engine and the engine compartment.

BRUSHES

Tire and wheel brushes: A heavy-bristle brush is recommended for tire cleaning. A softer scrub brush or a bottle brush is useful on wire or spoke wheels.

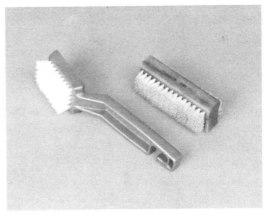

Scrub brushes: A small-size bristle brush is essential for scrubbing grit and grime from vinyl tops, upholstery, carpeting, etc. (You will see this type of brush used extensively in this book.)

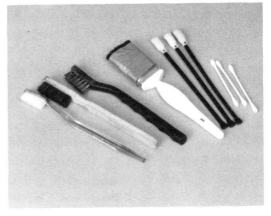

Detailing brushes and swabs: The brushes are used for removing wax residue from emblems, body seams, and hard-to-reach spots that your rag misses. The swabs (audio tape deck head cleaners or Q-Tips) are useful for reaching into air conditioning ducts to clean them.

APPLICATORS & TOWELS

Wax applicator pads: Used for applying carnauba wax or one-step products. Some come with the wax, others are available separately. We like the ones with terry-cloth covers, particularly for rubbing in a one-step cleaner-wax.

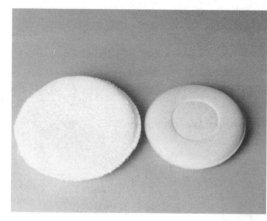

Liquid applicators: For applying rubber and vinyl protectant or glass cleaner. These eliminate overspray and reduce the amount of product you use. Available from auto suppliers and some supermarkets.

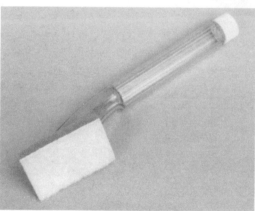

100% cotton terry-cloth towels, T-shirt rags, and window cleaning cloths: Get a dozen or so towels and T-shirt rags. (No graphics on the T-shirts, please.) For window cleaning, use lint-free turkish towels or cloths specifically designed for the job.

ELECTRIC ORBITAL BUFFER

Electric orbital buffer and bonnets: *These save time and are more gentle than cleaning and polishing by hand! You'll need at least 6 bonnets to do an average vehicle.*

PRO TIP: Should You Buy an Electric Orbital Buffer?

While a strong healthy person can get totally professional results cleaning and polishing paint by hand, we have found that an electric orbital butter is an extremely useful detailing tool. It offers these advantages: (1) it can save you an hour or two in paint cleaning and polishing time on every detail job, (2) it requires much less physical labor to get good results—especially when you are restoring badly weathered paint, (3) it is more gentle on the finish than hand rubbing, and (4) if you're physically not too strong, it will probably produce better results than you can by hand.

This type of orbital buffer is very easy to use. *On horizontal surfaces like this (which are always the most weathered), you can simply guide the buffer along, and let it do all the work. No pressure is required. The action is very gentle and easy to control.*

Here are answers to four of the most common questions about buffers:

1. What does a buffer cost, and is it "worth it?" A good quality orbital buffer costs $120 to $180. It is not a small purchase. With normal use, however, it will last for years. (We have one that's almost 15 years old!) Pay back is quick—doing just two detail jobs will pay for the buffer. (Ambitious readers might want to line up a few jobs with friends and family, and let *them* buy a buffer for you!)

2. Is a buffer hard to use? Years ago, all detailers used high-speed rotary-type buffers, often with wool bonnets. Some pros still use them. This type of buffer is a dangerous weapon in the hands of an unskilled worker. If too much pressure is applied, it can cut right through a paint job to bare metal. The cheapo buffer-driven-by-a-drill-motor can produce the same disastrous results. But the type of orbital buffer we show you here is, happily, much different. It doesn't apply torque or high-speed motion directly to the surface. Used with a non-abrasive cleaner, it is safe for clear-coat finishes.

3. What kind should I buy? First, make sure that it is a "random orbital buffer," intended for automotive use. This type is widely available at automotive parts stores, major department stores, hardware stores, etc. The buffer should have a soft sponge-like face pad. (You always use a soft 100% cotton terry-cloth bonnet over the pad.) We recommend a buffer with a 10- or 11-inch pad, that runs at a minimum of 2200 rpm. (The pad doesn't spin at that speed, but the orbital action does.)

4. What special accessories and supplies do I need? In addition to the buffer you'll need 6 or more bonnets. Bonnets are washed and dried after each use, and can last for a year or more. The same cleaners, polishes, and waxes that you would apply by hand are used with an orbital buffer. No special products are required.

See also the *Pro Tip: How to Use an Orbital Buffer* on page 57.

ASSEMBLING A PROPER WASHING KIT

Keep your kit in the bucket, ready to go at a moment's opportunity! This type of convenience will help you start quickly and get the job done in a very limited amount of time.

The kit starts with three items:

■ **A plastic wash bucket.** Two buckets are needed if you plan on not using a hose. Minimum 2-gallon capacity; 5-gallon is better. We prefer plastic to metal because it reduces the chance of scratching your vehicle. They also seem to be easier to keep clean.

■ **A good hose.** Since a car is 15 to 20 feet long, and it's pretty important to get all the way around it, buy at least a 50 footer. Add to that if it's a long distance from your water outlet to the shady place where you'll be washing. TIP: Make sure you have some soft hose washers so your hook-up can be water-tight.

■ **Hose nozzle.** We like the ones that shut off when you release them, because they reduce water usage and mess. This type is well suited to the technique taught in this book—washing and rinsing one section at a time.

Along with the above three items you will also need the following products. Which are discussed earlier in this Section.

■ **Wash mitt.** We recommend you buy two for faster washing.

■ **Chemical products:** Bug & tar remover, non-detergent car wash soap, spray-on/ hose-off wheel cleaner, tire cleaner, alcohol-based glass cleaner, etc.

■ **Brushes:** Both a stiff-bristle brush for tires and fender wells and softer scrub brushes for wheels.

■ **Chamois.** The *Pro Tip* on page 11 gives buying tips.

■ **Drying towels:** We like having a half a dozen smaller towels for two-handed work. Lint-free T-shirt rags, dish towels (also called "turkish towels"), or special industrial towels work best on window glass.

■ **Vacuum cleaner.** If you can get an extension cord to reach to your car or truck, your household vacuum will pull deep dirt better than a small automotive one.

ASSEMBLING A PROPER DETAILING KIT

Keep your detailing products and tools in a convenient box, ready to go. *If you know it's going to take a half hour to get things pulled together, there's a good chance you won't get started! Our plastic "milk crate" is nice, but a cardboard box also would work fine.*

In addition to the items in your wash kit, here's the additional items you should gather together in your detailing kit.

- **Chemical products:** cleaners, polish, wax, carpet shampoo, upholstery cleaner, rubber and vinyl protectant, leather conditioner, chrome and metal polish, plastic polish, engine cleaner, etc.

- **Detailing tools:** wax applicator pad, terry-cloth towels, detailing brushes and swabs, liquid protectant applicator, orbital buffer, bonnets, etc.

The key point is to keep your kit—whatever it contains—neatly assembled and ready to go.

KEEP THAT CLOTH CLEAN!

You'll find that the "kit" concept quickly goes to pot if you don't keep after your terry-cloth towels, T-shirt rags, window towels, and buffer bonnets. Our advice:

- **Wash after every use.** Toss your used towels, rags, and bonnets into the washer as soon as you're done working. That way your kit will be ready to go when you need it next time. TIP: Keep rags and bonnets that are discolored with paint oxidation in a separate load.

- **Use hot water and detergent in the wash.** *Do not use fabric softener!* It's not needed and it can inhibit the fabric's ability to absorb water. Hot water and detergent should remove all the chemicals and abrasives.

- **Don't use bleach.** It's normal for these towels, rags, and bonnets to get a bit stained.

- **Hang bonnets out to air dry.** An electric or gas dryer can ruin the elastic band.

A FINAL THOUGHT

The authors had some discussion on whether to include this advice on putting together kits. "After all, isn't it obvious that you should get this stuff organized?"

Well, it *wasn't* obvious. And after several times shagging things from various parts of the garage and the trunk of the car, we got out our bucket and milk crate, and got organized. The time savings in subsequent work was so substantial that we thought it warranted promotion to you.

Section 3:

Professional Automotive Hand Wash

INTRODUCTION

Washing a car is one of the easiest do-it-yourself automotive jobs. Nonetheless, we have chosen to give you a detailed step-by-step demonstration in this section for two reasons: (1) there *are* a few fine points to ensure quality that are not obvious otherwise, and (2) this is a great section to pass on to a young person you love who has never done the job before!

The wash job we describe here should take you about an hour. We assume you've assembled the wash kit described in Section 2, so you're ready to spring into action! A top-quality job includes not only washing and drying your car or truck, but vacuuming and dusting the interior, cleaning the glass, and applying protectant.

PREPARATION

Get ready: Put on comfortable clothes and shoes that won't mind a bit of water. Remove your belt buckle and watch to avoid scratching the finish.

Park in the shade and check hose reach. Hot direct sun can dry soap on the surface and cause water spotting. Make sure your hose can reach around the vehicle. HINT: Make sure there is a soft hose washer at every connection so you don't waste water. And check for drainage, so you don't end up working in a puddle!

Vacuum interior. It's easier to do before you get the area all wet. You don't want AC power cords in water. Besides, this keeps the extension cord and vacuum from getting muddy, which may make others in the household happy!

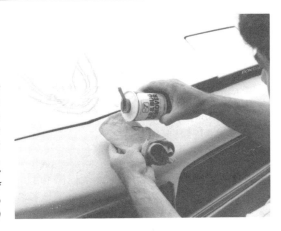

Apply Tar & Bug Remover as needed. *Use a terry-cloth rag to rub away the spots. This solvent-type chemical can remove road tar, tree sap, bird droppings, and sticky bugs. (HINT: This stuff removes wax, so use it sparingly.)*

Fill your bucket with 2 gallons of water. *Note how we've marked our bucket at the 2-gallon level so we always have the right amount of water.*

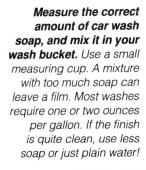

Measure the correct amount of car wash soap, and mix it in your wash bucket. *Use a small measuring cup. A mixture with too much soap can leave a film. Most washes require one or two ounces per gallon. If the finish is quite clean, use less soap or just plain water!*

PRO TIP: If You've Got Soft Water, Use It!

Many areas of the country have such hard water, that household water softeners are common. If you need a water softener *inside* your house for laundry, dishes, and bathing, why not use it on your car as well? Soft water will allow the soap to clean better, and it will reduce streaking and spotting.

If your house has a water softening system, it will usually bypass your outdoor garden hose spigot. To tap into soft water *inside* the house, attach a Y-connector (available from the hardware store) to a soft water line leading to your washing machine.

This simple, inexpensive Y-connector will allow you to "pipe" soft water to your driveway. *Use either Teflon tape or Teflon sealer on all the pipe and faucet threads to prevent water leaks.*

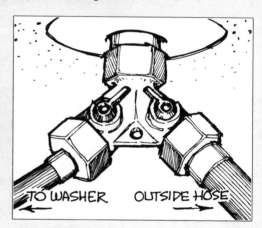

PRO TIP: How to Avoid a Wash Disaster

The biggest single cause of problems in hand washing is that people try to wash the whole car before rinsing it. The result is that the soap dries on the surface and causes streaks and spots. To avoid the problem, wash and rinse just one section of the vehicle at a time. Washing and rinsing in controllable sections is especially important on hot, dry days, when the soapy water dries fast.

PROPER WASHING

Visually divide your vehicle into at least 6 sections, which you will wash one at a time. *You will wash the upper sections before the lower ones. Let gravity help you move the dirt down and off!*

Rinse down the whole vehicle. *The purpose of this initial rinse is to remove as much dirt and dust as possible before you touch the surface with your wash mitt.*

Apply the appropriate wheel cleaner to the wheel in the section you are washing. *The choices are discussed on page 19. Let the wheel cleaner soak in while you wash the section. Don't let overspray get onto the paint.*

Begin washing each section at the highest point, and work your way downward. *What removes the dirt is rubbing your soapy mitt over every square inch of the vehicle's surface. Really get into all the corners and tight spots to do a good job.*

As you wash each section, be sure to overlap the borders. *This insures that no spots are left unwashed. Keep your mitt well soaked with your soapy solution.*

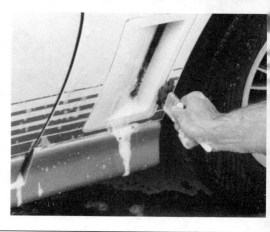

HINT: Clean small cracks that the wash mitt can't reach with a soft brush. *You want to remove every bit of visible dirt.*

IMPORTANT: Rinse each section as soon as it's washed. *Make sure the soap doesn't have any chance to dry on the paint and cause you problems.*

After rinsing the section, turn the nozzle to high pressure, and rinse out the wheel cleaning chemical. *These chemicals are extremely effective. Be sure not to splash any onto the paint. (You will go back for a final wash of the wheels and tires later.)*

The last sections you should wash are the lower areas. *These are the bumpers and below, the bottom half of the doors, and the areas around the wheels. This is where the most dirt accumulates.*

After washing the entire car, go back and do a final wash of just the wheels and tires. Use your soapy mitt on the wheels and your tire brush on the tires. You may need a second application of wheel cleaner. Clean whitewalls or discolored blackwalls as shown on page 94.

Also wash the fender wells as you do the wheels and tires. Your tire brush will work just fine. Get rid of all visible dirt for a first-class job.

Rinse off the tires and fender wells. Then give the whole car another complete rinse before you start drying it. By the way, if your rinse water doesn't bead up, the paint needs cleaning, polishing, and waxing, as described in Section 5.

PROPER DRYING

Begin drying immediately. You don't want any water to evaporate and leave spots. We like a two-step drying process: a quick first drying with a chamois to get rid of most of the water, followed by a final drying with dry soft terry-cloth towels to thoroughly eliminate all streaks. You can skip the chamois and do a terrific job with towels, but you'll need quite a pile of them. Before you begin, be sure to prepare your chamois by getting it soaking wet and very soft. Wring it out, and fold it over several times.

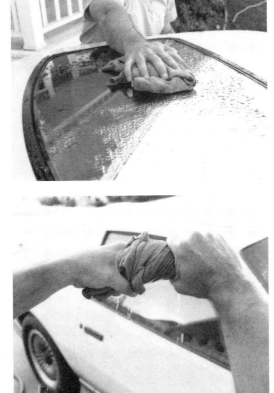

Dry the vehicle with your chamois, starting at the top. Work quickly on this first pass. Don't try to get the surface fully dry—just get rid of the big stuff. If you take more than 5 minutes for the whole vehicle, you're being too fussy on this first pass.

Squeeze out your chamois often! Give it a good twist, shake it out, and keep working.

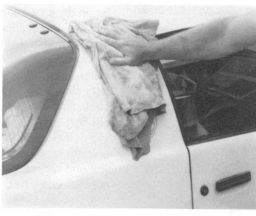

Make a second quick pass over the vehicle with your chamois. Continue to work quickly, since the final "detail" drying will be done with a towel.

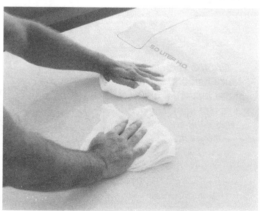

For the final drying, use a couple of clean terry-cloth towels. Put some elbow grease into the job at this point to buff out any water spots. Make sure the chrome is spotless. And don't forget to wipe down the windows.

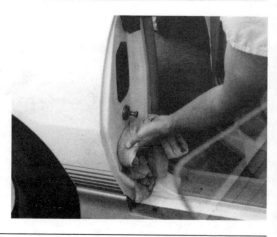

Open the doors, hood, and trunk, and dry the inside edges thoroughly. This is important to avoid drips and streaks.

PRO TIP: Water Spots—How to Remove Them

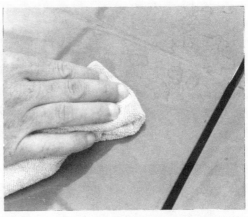

To remove water spots on a painted surface, use an appropriate cleaner and wax. *If you have clear-coat, be sure to use a non-abrasive product. Water spots often etch right through the wax, because each droplet acts like a magnifying glass. A one-step cleaner-wax can be useful here.*

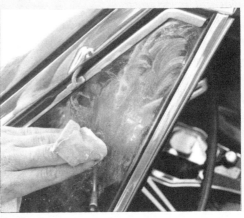

Water spots on glass may require a mild abrasive cleaner. *Here, the problem is the minerals from the water clinging to the glass, which the abrasive can remove.*

PRO TIP: Why the "Drive-to-Dry" Method Doesn't Work

We've all tried this—wash and rinse the car, jump in, and drive it (we won't say how fast) to dry it off! Nice concept—but it doesn't work. It leaves streaks in some places and water spots in others. You end up with a mess, and rather than saving time or effort, you get just the *opposite!*

GLASS CLEANING

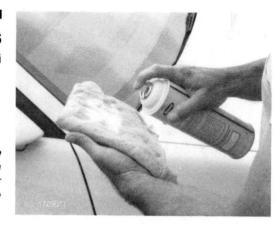

Apply spray-type cleaner to a cloth. *Then use the cloth to clean your windows. This technique prevents overspray.*

We recommend you try a liquid applicator for glass cleaner. *Alcohol-based cleaner works very nicely in this type of applicator. Rub the window until the surface feels slippery. Since glass cleaner can cut through your wax, this is a fast way to clean while avoiding overspray.*

Wipe the window dry with a lint-free cotton cloth, turning it often. *In a pinch, most types of newspaper will also work. But if it smears, it has water-based ink and shouldn't be used. Paper towels will dry the windows, but most leave lint.*

Most framed door windows should be dried at the top. *Roll the window down a few inches, dry it and the channel above it. Then roll the window back up and, if necessary, redry the lower part of the window.*

EXTERIOR FINISHING TOUCHES

Apply exterior rubber and vinyl protectant to the tires. *Use an applicator to avoid over-spray on the wheel. After the protectant soaks in for a minute or so, rub off the excess with a clean rag.*

Apply ERV protectant to any exterior rubber or vinyl trim. *Use the applicator or a small rag. Allow the protectant to soak in, then rub off excess with a cloth. Using protectant regularly is important to preserve the dark "color" of tires and trim.*

INTERIOR FINISHING

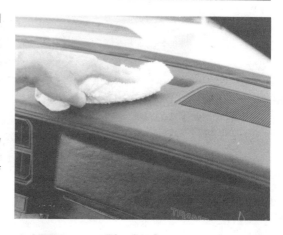

With a damp T-shirt rag, dust and clean all interior hard surfaces and vinyl or leather. *If necessary, use general-purpose cleaner on a rag for fingerprints.*

Finally, finish your wash job by cleaning the inside of the windows. *Be sure to get into all the tight corners for a first-class job.*

FINAL INSPECTION

Okay, if you've followed these instructions, you should have a nicely washed vehicle. Close the doors, and take a final walkaround with a towel in your hand to "fix" the inevitable water runs.

Hose off your mitts, rinse your bucket, toss the towels into the washing machine, and reassemble your wash kit, so you'll be ready to go next time. If you're proceeding with detailing, a good wash job is an essential first step.

Section 4:

Conserve Water: The Two-Bucket Wash

For the two-bucket wash you'll need the basic kit shown in Section 2, but with *two* buckets, *two* wash mitts, and no hose. You must read Section 3 for all the general techniques and *Pro Tips* on washing. This much shorter section focuses on the *differences* between washing with a hose versus two buckets.

This washing method offers two big advantages: (1) it can use as little as 5 gallons of water instead of 100 or more, and (2) it's perfect for those of you who can't get a hose to your vehicle. It can also be a preferred method for washing your car or truck inside your garage in the winter, where you don't want a lot of water splashing around.

**PROPER
WASHING**

Wash mitts are the key to success in the two-bucket wash. They hold both the wash water and the rinse water nicely and make the whole wash job go quickly as well. If you don't have mitts, use two small terry-cloth towels.

If your car or truck is really dirty, use a full bucket of wash solution (rather than just 2 gallons) and two or more full buckets of rinse water. If needed, apply Bug & Tar Remover before you begin.

Fill your wash bucket and rinse bucket. Use soft water, if available. Add the correct amount of automotive wash soap.

Use two mitts—one for wash soap and one for rinsing. Keep them separate throughout the procedure. Do not try to do this job with one mitt. (In a pinch, use two terry-cloth towels.)

RINSE MITT:
Wet down a section of
the car. *Each section should be about 1/6th of your vehicle, as shown on page 35. Use lots of water on this first pass. Start at the top of the section, and let the water "flow off" loose dust and dirt.*

WASH MITT:
Thoroughly wash the
wet section. *Make sure you cover every square inch. Pay special attention to trim, emblems, and hard-to-reach areas. If necessary, use a soft toothbrush on detail.*

RINSE MITT:
After washing each
section, rinse off all the
soap. *Again, start at the top of the section, and let gravity do some of the work for you. Make sure all the soap is off before proceeding to the next section. Never let soap dry on the surface.*

RINSE-WASH-RINSE:
Continue the 3-step process until you've washed all six sections of the vehicle. If your car or truck is really dirty, you may need to dump your rinse bucket halfway through and refill it.

WASH MITT:
Now go back and wash each of the wheels and tires. You may want to use a wheel cleaner to cut brake dust, rust, and oxidation (page 19).

BRUSH THEN RINSE MITT:
Scrub each tire, then rinse the entire wheel and tire. You may need a chemical cleaner on whitewalls (page 94). Repeat the process at each tire and wheel.

DRYING AND FINISHING

From here on, the two-bucket wash is the same as a conventional wash, since you don't need a hose for drying! But you do need another bucket of clean rinse water for wetting your chamois.

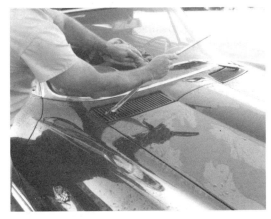

Dry the exterior, first with a chamois and then with dry terry-cloth towels. *Make sure you dry all the windows to prevent spots. Open the doors, hood, and trunk to dry inside the edges.*

Don't forget to dry the tires and vinyl or rubber trim and apply ERV protectant. *This is an essential part of a quality job.*

Use a clean, damp T-shirt rag to wipe down the interior. Remove all dust, fingerprints, and smudges from the dashboard, door panels, headliner, visors, and seats.

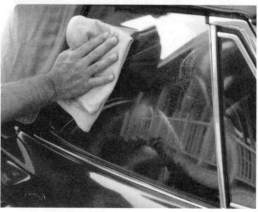

Clean the windows, inside and out, with automotive glass cleaner. Be sure to get into all the corners.

Even if you have a hose, you may find this a preferable method because of the water it saves.

Be sure to rinse your chamois, mitts, and buckets, so your wash kit will be ready to go next time.

Section 5:

Professional Paint Detailing

Paint cleaning, polishing, and waxing is one of the most satisfying and rewarding aspects of automotive detailing. Read Section 2 to learn what types of products are available and the basic three-step cleaning, polishing, and waxing process (*Pro Tip* on page 12).

This section presents four real-world case studies in paint detailing:

1. Badly weathered enamel paint

2. Normally weathered enamel paint

3. New clear-coat paint

4. Show-quality hand-rubbed lacquer

Detailing Cars & Trucks

BADLY WEATHERED ENAMEL PAINT

This 1978 Suburban was so badly oxidized that we seriously wondered whether we could restore it enough to use as an example in this book. Nonetheless, the alternative to our failure would be a paint job, so we were given the green light for a "full treatment." (If clear-coat paint is allowed to weather this badly, you can *count on* new paint being the only fix.) An electric orbital buffer is helpful for a case like this simply because it drastically reduces the work load. This is a real-world example of a minor miracle—and a big money-saver for the do-it-yourselfer!

BEFORE:
This old workhorse shows the rigors of benign neglect. After years of no more "detailing" than an occasional wash, the hood is so badly oxidized that it is totally dull and splotchy—no reflections at all!

AFTER:
This is what several hours of patient work with the right products and a three-step method can do. Notice the reflections of our canopy in the paint. It's hard to believe that this is the same truck!

Step 1: Clean

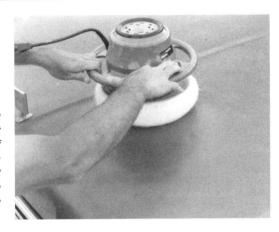

Always begin cleaning with a mild cleaner. Test it on a small area to see if it will remove the oxidation with a reasonable amount of time and effort. The idea is to remove as little paint as possible.

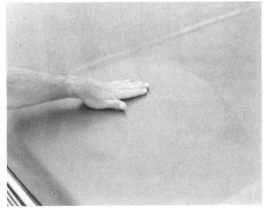

Check the results of the work done by the mild cleaner. Feel the area. If the cleaner is doing its job, the surface will feel smooth. Also, you should be able to see some shine at this point. Here the mild cleaner wasn't cutting the oxidation at all, so we moved up to something stronger.

The stronger cleaner shows improvement. The stronger abrasive does the job. Note: we're not using polishing or rubbing compound, just a heavy-duty cleaner. If, however, we were doing the job by hand, we would probably move up to polishing compound, just to make the job go faster. Use care with any compound because it can cut through paint quickly.

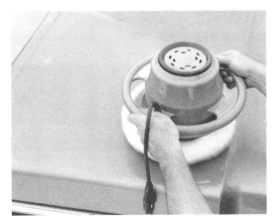

Clean ridges and valleys by hand. *The paint is thin on the tops of ridges, and it's easy to cut through the paint to the primer. Cleaning these areas by hand gives you more control and reduces the likelihood of damaging the paint. Also, hand-clean areas the buffer won't reach, like under door handles and next to badges and trim.*

Here you can see the contrast between the cleaned side and the oxidized side of the hood. *Through this case study we're focusing on the hood, which was the worst part of the vehicle. (We're three buffer bonnets into the job at this point!)*

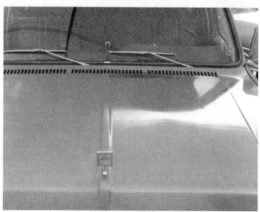

Step 2: Polish

Use a clean bonnet or cloth, and apply a small amount of polish. *Work the polish into the surface until it dries. Then keep working with a fresh buffer bonnet or cloth to pick up all the polish residue and deepen the shine.*

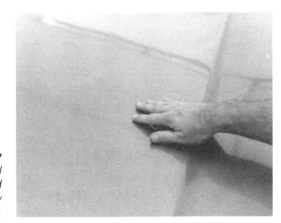

Check the surface by hand. It should feel uniformly smooth and slippery. If not, apply another coat of polish.

Here, we applied and buffed out an ultrafine polish. This fills scratches and swirls and adds further luster to the paint.

Step 3: Wax

Apply a thin film of carnauba wax by hand. Here's another of those situations where more is not better. Use the wax sparingly, or it will be difficult to buff out. Do not use a power buffer to apply wax.

Allow the wax to harden.
This could take from 10 minutes to a half hour, depending on the air temperature and the thickness of the wax. It's ready to buff when it has turned "cloudy."

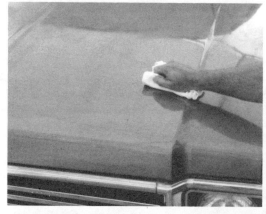

Buff the wax by hand with a fresh cotton cloth.
Fold the rag into a firm pad, and turn it often to expose a fresh surface as you buff. Again, do NOT use a power buffer.

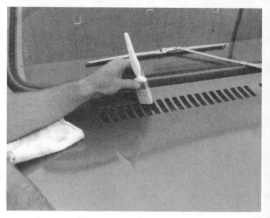

Remove polish and wax residue. Clean it out of all grilles, seams, and joints, and from around the emblems. (See page 52 for the finished hood.)

PRO TIP: How to Use an Orbital Buffer

Make sure the elastic band of the bonnet fits into the recessed groove in the buffer's head. This keeps the bonnet in place and allows the head to spin freely.

Never bear down on the buffer. Allow the pad to move freely. Your hands should merely guide the buffer around. The buffer should do the work for you, so don't make the job tougher than it needs to be.

Wherever possible, keep the full head in contact with the paint surface. That way it's working to maximum efficiency.

CONVENTIONAL PAINT (NON-CLEAR-COAT)

The subject of this paint detailing project is a well-cared-for 1974 Oldsmobile convertible. Like most older cars, the finish is conventional paint with no protective clear-coat.

The car is washed weekly and gets a quarterly paint detailing like the one described here. Clearly, the care has paid off. Little effort is required to keep this car looking great, despite the fact that it's never garaged! This "case study" is very typical: a normally weathered daily driver.

BEFORE:
The well-maintained paint on this Olds looks okay. Just a normal paint detailing job is required— no miracles needed.

AFTER:
Four hours work with the right products has this old smile-maker looking great and protected for another three to four months.

Step 1: Clean

Apply a small amount of cleaner to the buffer bonnet. *Cleaning a normally weathered finish like this can be done equally well by hand. We chose to use a non-abrasive cleaner—the same product you would also use on a clear-coat finish.*

Work on an area about 3 feet square. *Keep the buffer moving, and work the surface until the cleaner disappears. If working by hand, do not apply too much pressure.*

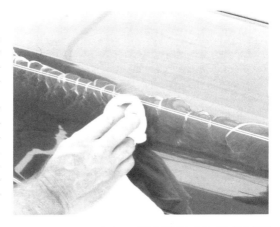

Go easy on pinstriping and ridges. *Even a mild cleaner with light abrasives can wear through the thin paint on ridge tops. Also hand clean areas the buffer won't reach, like under door handles and next to badges and trim. Check the surface by hand. It should feel uniformly smooth and slippery.*

Detailing Cars & Trucks

Gently touch up any rough spots. *Use a clean terry-cloth rag and a small amount of cleaner.*

Step 2: Polish

Polish the cleaned surface. *Use a clean bonnet or cloth and a small amount of polish. Work the surface until the polish dries. Then switch to a fresh buffer bonnet or cloth, and buff until all the residue is removed and the surface is shiny.*

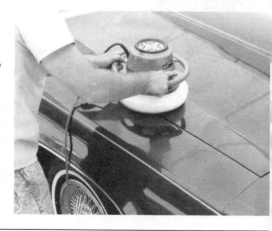

For a deeper shine, we applied a second coat of polish. *For maximum "glazing" effectiveness, apply the polish, but don't buff it off. Let it stand for at least 10 minutes to allow the resins to soak in and fill the "spider webbing." If you wish, you could use an ultrafine "glaze" for this step.*

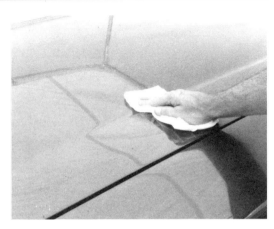

Hand buff the final coat of polish or glaze. *We think this is the best part of paint detailing— watching the final luster show up as the polish residue is removed from the final glaze!*

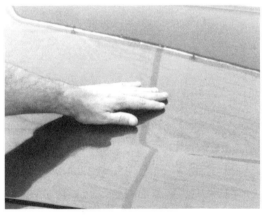

Do one final inspection of the polished surface before applying wax. *This is the time to take care of any lingering bits of roughness that you might have missed. At this point, the surface should be perfect.*

Step 3: Wax

Apply a thin film of carnauba wax by hand. *Use only a small amount of wax on the applicator pad, and spread it evenly.*

Allow the wax to harden.
This can take up to half an hour, depending on the air temperature and how much wax you applied. When it's cloudy like this, it's ready to buff out.

Buff the wax by hand with a fresh cloth. Fold the rag into a firm pad, and turn it often to expose a fresh surface as you buff.

Remove polish and wax residue. Clean it out of all nooks and crannies, seams, and joints, and from around the emblems. See the Pro Tip on page 73.

CLEAR-COAT PAINT

The subject of this paint detailing project is a clear-coat black metallic finish on a new '91 Acura. Before delivery, this vehicle was "detailed" with one-step cleaner-wax and a high-speed rotary buffer. The result was a lot of swirl marks that were particularly visible in direct sunlight.

One of our goals in this paint-detailing "case study" was to remove those swirl marks using ultrafine glaze. The other goal was to demonstrate detailing on a most demanding color: clear-coat black.

BEFORE:
Despite being clean and new, the black clear-coat finish on this '91 Acura lacks depth and brilliance.

AFTER:
This is what a black car is supposed to look like! Even in direct sunlight, the finish looks wet and shows no signs of the spider webbing created by a high-speed rotary buffer.

Detailing Cars & Trucks

Step 1: Clean

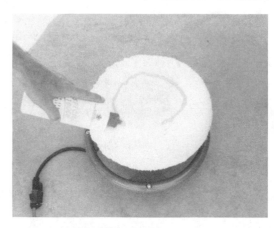

Apply a small amount of non-abrasive cleaner to the buffer bonnet. This is a relatively clean surface, so you won't need much cleaner. This step, like the other ones in this procedure, can be done by hand with equally good results.

Work on an area about 3 feet square. Keep the buffer moving, and work the surface until the cleaner disappears. Check the surface by hand. It should feel uniformly smooth and slippery.

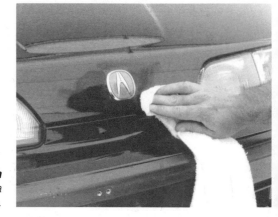

Clean hard-to-reach spots by hand. Use a clean cotton cloth.

Step 2: Polish

Apply polish to the cleaned surface. *Use a clean bonnet and a small amount of polish. Work the polish into the surface.*

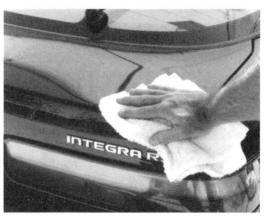

Buff the polish by hand. *Fold a clean terry-cloth towel into a pad, and rub the surface with even pressure. Turn the towel often to keep the polish residue from building up on the paint.*

"Glaze" the surface with a scratch-filling ultrafine polish. *Use another fresh bonnet on the buffer. Apply the polish with the buffer, and let it sit for at least 10 minutes to allow the resins to soak in and fill the "spider webbing."*

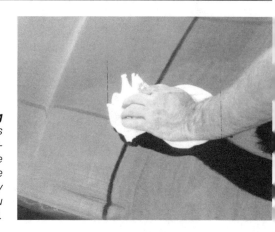

Hand buff the glazing polish. The finish is starting to look spectacular! Inspect the polished surface before applying wax. Correct any roughness or spots you might have missed.

Step 3: Wax

Apply a thin coat of carnauba wax by hand. Use only a little wax on the applicator pad, and spread it evenly so it will be easy to buff.

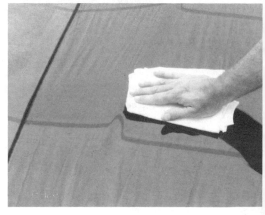

After the wax hardens, buff it by hand. Fold a fresh cloth into a pad, and turn it often as you buff. We removed all wax residue as shown in the Pro Tip on page 73. (The finished car is shown on page 63.)

SHOW-QUALITY LACQUER PAINT

The subject of this paint detailing project is a restored show-quality 1965 Corvette. The body was taken down to bare fiberglass, block-sanded to remove all waviness from the factory molds, resealed, primered, and painted with multiple coats of wet-sanded and hand-rubbed red lacquer.

This paint job is representative of the very finest non-clear-coat available. It is also typical of what you will find on many exotics and show cars today. We thought it would be an interesting "case study" for you to see.

BEFORE:
This car has led a totally sheltered life since restoration. Most people would ask "Are you guys crazy? This finish is beautiful. It doesn't need detailing."

AFTER:
You can't see the difference in a photo. But you can feel it! The finish is now sensuously smooth to the touch. The gloss is deeper and the shine perfect. This is what judges like to feel— perfection!

Detailing Cars & Trucks

Step 1: Clean

Apply a small amount of mild non-abrasive cleaner to a bonnet or a *clean terry-cloth rag. Although this car does not have a clear-coat, the show-quality lacquer requires only a very light cleaning.*

Apply cleaner to a small area, about 3 square feet. The surface will get cloudy at first, then as you continue to buff, it will clear and begin to shine.

Clean low spots, ridges, and peaks by hand, using a terry-cloth towel and the same cleaner. Be careful: you can apply more pressure with your hand than you can with a buffer.

Clean by hand all areas where the buffer can't reach. *This includes the areas under door handles, around the antenna, and other hard-to-reach spots.*

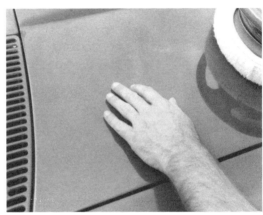

Lightly run your fingertips across the surface to check your progress. *Don't trust your eyes. Correct cleaning produces an extremely slippery, "grain-free" feel. If it looks clean but doesn't feel clean, it's not clean! If necessary, reapply cleaner until the surface is perfectly smooth.*

Step 2: Polish

Apply polish to a clean bonnet or terry-cloth rag. *Use about half as much polish as cleaner.*

Apply polish to the entire vehicle. *It will leave a cloudy film. Wait about 10 minutes for it to soak in.*

Buff the polish with a clean bonnet or terry-cloth towel. *Even though we started with a pampered finish, we produced a big difference in the shine.*

Apply ultrafine polish. *At this level of quality, an ultimate "glaze" is essential for a wet-look finish. It is especially important with red or black paint. Let it sit for 10 minutes.*

Buff the ultrafine polish by hand. *Use a clean soft rag to make sure that every bit of residue is off.*

Final quality check. *This is the last chance to make sure the finish is perfect before applying wax.*

Step 3: Wax

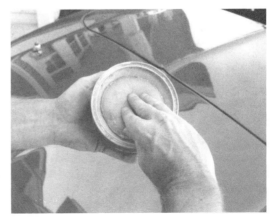

Put a very small amount of wax on a pad applicator. *Again, don't make the mistake of thinking "more is better." It's not.*

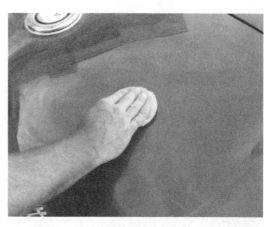

Apply the wax thoroughly and evenly. *Don't leave any "holes" in your application. Let the wax dry to a white powder. Don't worry about getting wax in emblems and cracks. You will remove it later.*

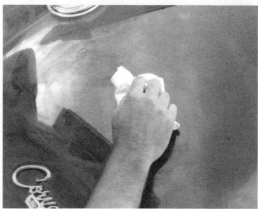

Buff the wax with a clean terry-cloth towel or T-shirt rag. *Turn the cloth often. If the wax is difficult to buff, you applied too much—use less the next time.*

The *Pro Tip* on the facing page gives you an idea of the attention you should pay to removing *all* wax residue—especially for show-quality results.

Once the paint is finished, you will need to invest several more hours of satisfying work in detailing the trim, tires, wheels, and interior of your car or truck. For show-quality work, you'll also want to do the trunk or bed, underhood, and chassis.

PRO TIP: Detailing the Details

A good friend who is the editor of an automotive magazine and is often a judge at concourse d'elegance events told us "what really sets off the amateur detailing jobs is the ugly white wax residue in the tiny tight spots. These guys think 99.9% is good enough. But that residue is just like a badge that says lazy... The most important 30 minutes in a detail job is getting rid of that stuff." Here's how:

For cleaning around emblems and trim, prepare a clean, dry paint brush for the job. Wrap it in masking tape, leaving only the lower quarter-inch exposed. We've found this is a most effective tool.

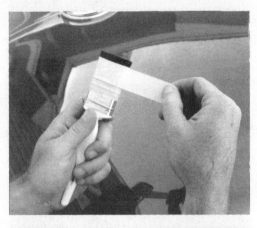

Use the paint brush to clean the dried wax residue out of raised emblems. A quick brushing action gets the job done fast. Use the whole surface of the brush.

You may need a stiffer toothbrush or detailing brush for stubborn wax residue. *Cleaning out dried wax is critically important for top results.*

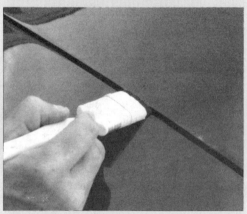

Use the paint brush to remove wax from cracks where body panels meet. *Take your time and do this job right. Make sure no wax residue can be seen—even when the doors, trunk, and hood are open.*

A correctly detailed emblem. *Notice that no wax residue can be seen anywhere. A Q-Tip also works well for getting loosened residue out of corners. Pros gauge the efforts of others by such details.*

Section 6:
Trim Detailing

Thirty years ago, all automotive trim was chrome-plated metal. It was pretty, but prone to rust. Designers today use a variety of materials to achieve the "look" they want. Since trim is an important accent in the design of your car or truck, it deserves special attention. This section shows you how to detail the four major types of trim:

1. **Chrome-plated metal.** Chromium itself is extremely hard but thin, and the metal it covers is prone to rust. Once the chrome surface has been broken through by a scratch or rust, it will need special care for the rest of the life of the vehicle. Chemical chrome cleaners work well on chrome that's in good condition, but if it has

surface rust, we recommend chrome or metal polish with a mild abrasive. Wax should always be applied to chrome to retard rust.

2. **Chrome-plated plastic.** This has been used extensively on cars and trucks over the past 20 years. This type of chrome trim is much more delicate, but at least is not subject to rusting. It should be cleaned with plastic polish—a very mild cleaner. *CAUTION: Standard chrome polish or metal polish can ruin plastic chrome.* We show you how to tell the difference in this section. Wax is not needed on plastic chrome trim.

3. **Aluminum and stainless steel.** There is a decreasing use of these metals on newer vehicles. To protect against corrosion, aluminum trim is often treated with a chemical process ("anodizing") or is coated with clear acrylic plastic. Harsh abrasive can "cloud" the anodized or clear-coated finish on aluminum trim and still not improve the shine, and should be avoided. Plastic polish works well on such surfaces. Bare, unprotected aluminum may become quite discolored with surface corrosion, but it can be easily cleaned and restored with metal polish. Stainless steel is always uncoated, and it can be nicely cleaned with metal polish.

4. **Vinyl and rubber.** These types of trim are cleaned with vinyl cleaner, tire cleaner, or all-purpose cleaner. Be sure to apply exterior rubber and vinyl (ERV) protectant to restore color and sheen.

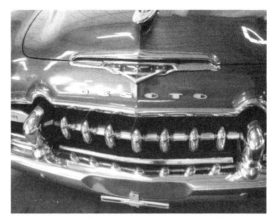

Most old classics use only chrome for trim, like this DeSoto. An hour or so with chrome or metal polish keeps it bright and shiny. Most chrome polish has a mild abrasive and strong chemicals to get rid of surface rust.

Most late-model cars and trucks are adorned with several types of trim. Happily, most of the plastic trim pieces on this new Acura can be detailed with plastic polish. The only other chemical required is ERV for the soft contact strip in the bumpers and on the sides.

PRO TIP: Don't Use It Until You Knock It

Those wonderful metal polishes that so easily restore luster to chrome-plated *metal* trim will just as easily remove the chrome-like finish from *plastic* trim. So, how do you tell whether a piece of trim is chrome-plated metal or vacuum-metalized plastic? We find that *sound* is the best indicator. Just tap a trim piece with a small metal object, such as the blade of a small screwdriver, and listen to the sound. Metal trim pieces, including pot metal, will almost invariably emit a metallic ringing sound, but plastic won't. (A magnet is not a reliable indicator, because some "pot metal" trim is non-magnetic.)

CHROME-PLATED METAL TRIM

For chrome that's in good condition, use a little chrome or metal polish on a clean cloth. Polish with light pressure, and remove all cleaner residue. Then, protect the chrome with carnauba wax.

Remove surface rust from neglected chrome with chrome cleaner, a stiff brush, and elbow grease. Don't use steel wool, or you will further damage the chrome and cause it to rust even faster.

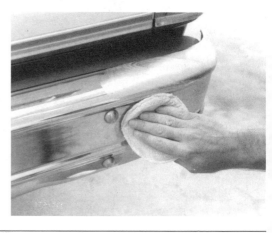

Polish the chrome to restore its shine, and remove the residue with a clean cloth. Then, protect the chrome with carnauba wax.

CHROME-PLATED PLASTIC TRIM

Use plastic polish on all chrome-plated plastic trim. This trunk emblem looks like regular chrome trim, but it's really plated plastic and must be cleaned with mild plastic polish.

Chrome-plated plastic trim can be easily damaged. This piece was accidentally cleaned with regular chrome polish—an easy mistake. If you're not sure what type trim you have, tap it and listen to the sound. Chrome-plated metal has a distinctive metallic sound; plastic does not.

In spite of what it looks like, this grille is chrome-plated plastic—not metal. Trim pieces like this were becoming common when this car was made, nearly two decades ago. However, periodic cleaning with non-abrasive plastic polish has kept the grille looking new.

PAINTED PLASTIC TRIM

Clean plastic mirror bodies like this one with plastic cleaner. *We've also given it some depth—and protection—with a light wipe of ERV protectant.*

Remove oxidation from plastic bumpers with plastic polish. *Regular paint cleaner can be too strong or abrasive for the soft plastic finish. The oxidation was removed from the end of this black plastic bumper facia with plastic polish. Note the difference between the treated and untreated portions!*

Painted plastic body extensions should also be cleaned with plastic polish and protected with ERV. *These may look like painted metal, but they are actually painted flexible plastic. Additives in the paint allow it to flex with the plastic, and reduce the paint's hardness.*

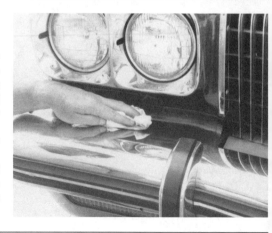

ALUMINUM & STAINLESS TRIM

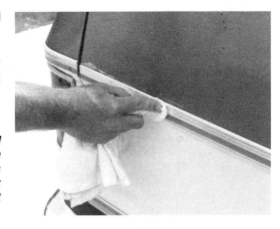

Clean aluminum and stainless steel trim with metal polish. *Polishes like Simichrome or Flitz work well. Clean paint accents with plastic polish.*

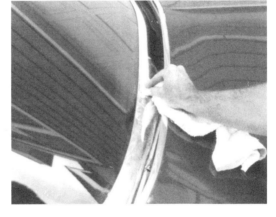

Mirror-finished stainless trim like this windshield molding is cleaned with metal polish. *Either a very-fine abrasive or non-abrasive type works well to restore the mirror-like surface.*

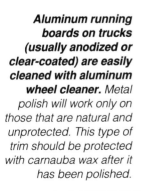

Aluminum running boards on trucks (usually anodized or clear-coated) are easily cleaned with aluminum wheel cleaner. *Metal polish will work only on those that are natural and unprotected. This type of trim should be protected with carnauba wax after it has been polished.*

RUBBER AND VINYL TRIM

Treat the rubber molding on bumpers with exterior rubber and vinyl (ERV) protectant. *The black color is an accent in the vehicle design, and the protectant makes it stand out.*

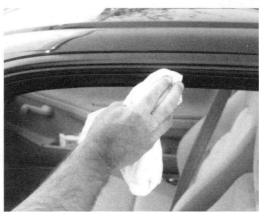

Apply ERV protectant to door weather stripping. *This keeps it supple and prevents it from cracking. The protectant also provides "lubrication" that will usually stop annoying squeaks from glass against the molding.*

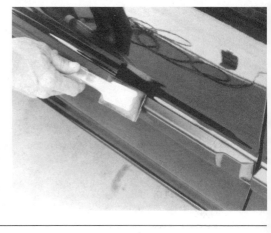

Apply ERV protectant to all exterior rubber and vinyl trim. *It restores the depth of color and contrast to these pieces.*

HOW TO RESTORE TRIM BACKGROUND COLOR

You can make shabby badges like this one look new. *All it takes is some automotive touch-up paint or plastic model airplane paint and a steady hand.*

Clean the badge with wax-and-silicone remover. *This ensures that the paint will adhere.*

Apply the paint to the background with a small artist's brush. *For the black background inside the letters we used Testor's Flat Black purchased at a model shop. The gold background was restored with automotive touch-up paint.*

Clean excess paint off of the face of the badge with thinner. *Wait until the paint is dry. Then, wipe the paint off of the edges with a clean rag containing only a small amount of thinner. If the rag is too damp, the thinner will wash the fresh paint out of the badge.*

A restored badge—good as new. *This complements the paint detail work on this Chevy Suburban (page 52).*

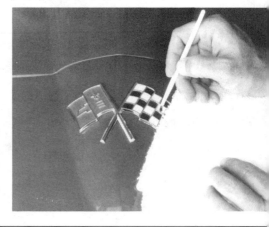

The enamel background colors in this Corvette emblem require high-gloss paint. *Flow the paint into the background to avoid brush strokes.*

HOW TO RESTORE CHROME TRIM ON PLASTIC

The thin accent lines on this taillight lens, worn away by countless wash jobs, can be quickly renewed with automotive or modeler's "chrome" paint.

Repaint the accents in smooth, continuous strokes. Clean the surface with wax-and-silicone remover. Shake the paint from time to time to thoroughly mix the metallic particles.

A couple of minutes and less than two dollars in paint brought these taillight lenses back to life. Although not perfect, this paint works much better than you might expect.

Here's one we've all seen—"chrome" accents worn off of a plastic instrument panel. *Use the same procedure as we did with the taillight lens on the preceding page. Clean the panel with wax-and-silicone remover.*

Paint the accent lines with smooth, continuous strokes. *On raised numbers and words, lightly "dry-brush" over the tops with very little paint on the brush. Use light, quick strokes.*

A simple "restoration" of this instrument panel was achieved in under an hour for less than a dollar! *The absolutely correct approach requires hours to remove and disassemble the panel, have it replated (about $50), repaint the background, then reassemble and reinstall it.*

Section 7:

Convertible Top Detailing

INTRODUCTION

Convertible tops require a bit of special attention every time they are washed. This short section focuses on a few tricks for cleaning and preserving them. If your top is really shot, only a new one will make your car look first-rate. But if your top is in pretty good condition, we show you here the extra work that is required to keep it that way. We also show you the special care you must give to a flexible plastic window. Most convertible tops are vinyl-coated canvas, which you see here. If you have a European car with a cloth top, see the *Pro Tip* on page 89.

NOTE: If your car has a padded vinyl top or a "faux" convertible top, these instructions apply equally well.

CLEANING VINYL TOPS

Use vinyl upholstery shampoo to clean a dirty convertible top. This product is considerably stronger than the wash soap in your bucket. Use aerosol foam shampoo right out of the can.

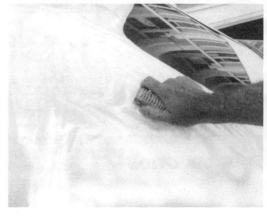

Use a stiff brush to work the shampoo into the grain of the fabric. You must use a brush to get a top really clean. A rag just won't work nearly as well.

Pay special attention to seams and crevices. A toothbrush works great for cleaning along welts and down in cracks.

Wipe off the shampoo, and check your work. *Once the top is dry, look for spots you may have missed, and clean these again. Then, dry the entire top with a clean terry-cloth towel.*

Apply exterior rubber and vinyl (ERV) protectant to the vinyl-coated top. *Allow the protectant to sit for several minutes before "buffing" off the excess. This treatment protects the vinyl and makes it tougher for dirt and grime to grab hold.*

PRO TIP: Cleaning European Cloth Tops

The lovely cloth tops on many European cars do not have a vinyl coating. Several manufacturers we contacted said that fabric upholstery shampoo worked well, but several would recommend only their own factory-brand products (at prices as high as $75). If you have a vehicle with such a top, we recommend you follow factory advice for the sake of safety and warranty protection. If your vehicle is out of warranty, you may wish to experiment with mild shampoo on a hidden surface. (Of course, one rep said the best action was to keep the top out of the rain! Hmmm...)

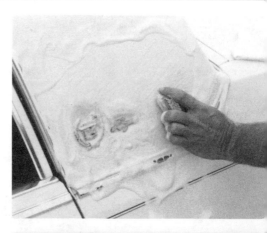

Clean a padded vinyl top just like a vinyl-coated convertible top. *Use vinyl shampoo and a brush, as shown on the preceding pages.*

Don't forget the frame and bows inside a convertible top. *Use a cleaner and wax appropriate for the finish.*

Open the top and clean the top of the windshield and the mating edge of the top. *This area is usually overlooked, yet it must be detailed for great "top-down" looks.*

Polish chrome latches and trim. *These hold-down latches and the area around them can collect a fair amount of dirt if the top is lowered very often.*

CLEANING PLASTIC WINDOWS

This plastic rear window has a large water stain. *Plastic polish and careful rubbing are required to remove the stain without damaging the tender plastic.*

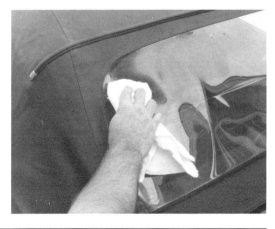

Apply plastic polish with a clean terry-cloth towel. *Lightly rub the surface with the polish, and then buff it to a clear shine. Once the spot has been removed, clean the rest of the window with plastic polish.*

The finished, detailed window. *The spot is gone and the window looks like new!*

Section 8:

Professional Tire & Wheel Detailing

During washing, tires and wheels are each cleaned with specialized products. This section shows you how to select and use these "spray-on hose-off" time-savers. The acid-wash type wheel cleaners cut rust and oxidation effectively, and the general-purpose wheel cleaners are good for road grime and brake dust. But there are no simple short cuts for making tires and wheels look great. At the finest level of detailing, it's good old elbow grease, the correct polish, a terry-cloth rag over your index finger, and a small brush that will produce a perfect wheel and tire! In this section we set you in the right direction, based on the type of wheel you have, and then take you through some typical wheel detailing "case studies."

TIRE DETAILING

As you begin a wash job, spray tire cleaner on the dry tire. *Whitewall tire cleaner works equally well on blackwalls.*

Scrub the sidewall with a stiff tire brush. *Be sure to get into the crevice where the tire meets the wheel.*

Rinse the tire and wheel thoroughly. *Then, after you've washed and dried the rest of the vehicle, towel off any water that remains on the tire.*

Apply exterior rubber and vinyl (ERV) protectant to the tire, starting from the center and working outward. *Be sure to totally cover the side of the tread. Buff the tire with a clean, dry rag to even out the protectant. Really weathered tires may need several applications.*

Don't spray ERV protectant directly on the tire—*it gets on the wheel and paint too easily. If you don't have an applicator, spray ERV on a rag and then apply it to the tire.*

PRO TIP: Use an Applicator

This type of liquid applicator is useful for ERV protectant and for window cleaner. *It applies the right amount, avoids overspray, and does a faster job of applying the product.*

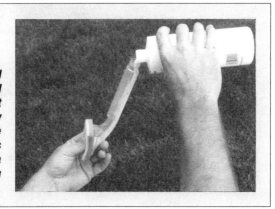

A CLEANING PLAN FOR YOUR WHEELS

We offer the following visual guide to give you a starting point for determining the cleaning needs of *your* wheels. These are typical examples. If you are not *absolutely sure* about what type of wheels you have, just remember that the general-purpose type of wheel cleaners are safe for all wheels. *CAUTION: Before using acid-wash products, make sure you have the correct product for your wheels, and read the manufacturer's warnings carefully.* Also, be sure to use the correct type of polish: chrome, metal, or plastic. Here's a wheel-by-wheel rundown:

Plastic wheel covers: Wash with an all-purpose wheel cleaner to remove grime. Shine with plastic polish. Protect with wax.

Cast-aluminum wheels with metallic paint or clear-coat: Wash with all-purpose wheel cleaner. Shine with plastic polish. (Why plastic polish? Because the outermost surface is clear-coat, not metal.) Protect with wax.

Aluminum wheels with clear-coat: *Wash with all-purpose wheel cleaner. Shine with plastic polish. Protect with wax.*

Painted wheels with chrome and stainless caps and rings: *Remove trim ring and center cap. Wash with all-purpose wheel cleaner. Touch up paint with appropriate color, and protect with wax. Shine trim ring and cap with chrome polish, and protect with wax.*

Chrome-plated and polished stainless-steel hubcaps: *Wash with all-purpose wheel cleaner. Shine with chrome polish (avoid painted accents). Protect with wax.*

Polished aluminum wheels—no clear-coat: *Wash with mild aluminum wash for polished and anodized wheels. Shine with metal polish. Protect with wax.*

Natural unpolished cast-aluminum wheels—no clear-coat: *Wash and deep clean with acid-base aluminum wheel cleaner. Because of their rough texture, shining or waxing is very difficult.*

Chrome-plated and stainless wire-wheel covers: *Wash with chrome and wire wheel cover cleaner. Shine with chrome polish. Protect with wax.*

Chrome-plated styled steel wheels: *Wash and remove light surface rust with acid-base chrome wheel cleaner. Shine with chrome polish. Protect with wax.*

Chrome-plated aluminum wheels: *Wash and clean with chrome and wire wheel cleaner. Carefully follow the manufacturer's instructions to avoid damaging your wheels. Protect with wax.*

Chrome-plated real wire wheels: *Wash and clean with chrome and wire wheel cleaner. Carefully follow the manufacturer's instructions to avoid damaging your wheels. Protect with wax.*

Detailing Cars & Trucks

HOW TO DETAIL CHROME WHEELS

This chrome-plated truck wheel has developed a serious rust problem. Both the center of the wheel and the hub cover have been infected by the "red cancer."

Spray chrome and wire wheel cleaner on the wheel. Protect your eyes with safety goggles, and keep the acid-based cleaner off of your skin and clothing. (We use spray-on hose-off wheel cleaner at the same time we're washing the whole vehicle.)

Scrub rusty areas with a toothbrush to remove scale. Don't use a wire brush; it will scratch the chrome and encourage even more rust.

Rinse the wheel with clear water to neutralize the wheel cleaner. *Flush the wheel thoroughly to make sure all the cleaner has been removed. We cleaned and rinsed the other three wheels the same way. (If the product you are using includes a neutralizer chemical, be sure to apply it.)*

Polish the wheel, wax it, and remove any residue with a toothbrush. *Use chrome polish or metal polish on a terry-cloth rag. Carnauba wax will help retard the rusting.*

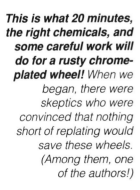

This is what 20 minutes, the right chemicals, and some careful work will do for a rusty chrome-plated wheel! *When we began, there were skeptics who were convinced that nothing short of replating would save these wheels. (Among them, one of the authors!)*

HOW TO DETAIL PAINTED WHEELS

Painted wheels with chrome caps and trim rings require disassembly for proper detailing. *Remove the caps and rings carefully to avoid damage to them or injury to yourself.*

Clean the wheel with all-purpose wheel cleaner. *Clean tight spots with a stiff brush. Clean the tire as described on page 94. Thoroughly dry the wheel and tire, but don't put ERV on the tire yet, as it could cause problems if any touch-up painting is needed on the wheel.*

If touch-up is required, spray the wheel with the appropriate color. *Use a cardboard paint block to keep overspray off of the tire. Mask the valve stem to prevent it from getting painted, and clean the wheel with wax-and-silicone remover before painting.*

Clean the center cap and trim ring with chrome or metal polish. *Then, protect them with a coat of carnauba wax, and install them on the wheel once the paint is completely dry. We prefer to wait overnight before installing the caps and rings to give the paint a chance to thoroughly dry.*

Install the ring and center cap by hand. *Protect the trim pieces— and your hands—with a soft, clean cloth folded into a pad. (ERV was applied to the tire before the trim pieces were installed to eliminate any mess.)*

This wheel looks as good as it did when it rolled off of a GM assembly line in 1968. *And it required less than 1/2 hour of detailing!*

HOW TO DETAIL WIRE WHEELS AND COVERS

Spray on chrome and wire wheel cleaner. *Be sure to read the manufacturer's instructions and warnings. This is an effective but strong acid-type cleaner.*

Scrub the cleaner into rust spots to remove scaling. *Be sure to wear goggles. Rust usually appears first at the ends of the spokes.*

Hose off the cleaner. *If a neutralizer chemical was supplied with your wheel cleaner, be sure to use it. Flush the wheel thoroughly with water.*

Polish the wheel with chrome or metal polish. *We would love to give you a keen shortcut here—but we don't know any. Polishing is going to take you some time. Apply a coat of wax to retard rusting.*

Remove all polish and wax residue. *Clean up with a small stiff brush.*

The procedure for cleaning and detailing a wire wheel cover is no different. *Do check carefully the intended application of your acid-wash product, however, since some product lines have a milder acid-wash for wire wheel covers. (This is because some covers include parts that are not chrome-plated steel.)*

WHEEL-WELL DETAILING

Wheel wells "frame" the wheels. Here's a case study of an enthusiast approach to the job. CAUTION: Use jack stands to safely support the vehicle, and chock the opposite wheels.

Rinse the fender well with a high-pressure hose, and then scrub it with a mixture of all-purpose cleaner and water. Scrub the suspension and steering, brake caliper, etc. Avoid getting soap or water into the engine area.

Thoroughly rinse and dry the entire wheel well and suspension. To avoid rust, make sure the brake rotor is thoroughly dry.

If necessary, spray low-gloss black paint on the inside of the wheel well. *Be careful not to get overspray on the outside of the vehicle.*

If necessary, spray the suspension components with appropriate paint. *Use a cardboard paint block to avoid overspray. If you get any paint on bolt heads, wipe it off immediately with a rag. Apply ERV protectant to brake hoses and any other rubber parts.*

The finished wheel well area. *The black portions are really black—and the entire area is clean. Yes, this is fastidious attention to detail, but this car also has won a "best undercarriage" trophy because of it!*

TOUCHING UP WHEEL COVER ACCENTS

This before-and-after comparison shows the results of some careful painting. *The paint accents on these 1965 Corvette wheel covers were looking pretty bad!*

Mask the accent areas and spray with paint of the correct type and color. *Be sure to prepare the surface with wax-and-silicone remover to assure good bonding. Spray several very light coats of paint.*

Here's the real payoff! *A detailed wheel cover in a detailed wheel well on a detailed Corvette. The wheel cover was protected with a fresh coat of carnauba wax. It looks as good as it did when it was new—26 years ago!*

Section 9:

Professional Interior Detailing

Interior detailing is just as important as the exterior. After all, this is where *you* spend most of your time! A major failing of many amateur jobs is the lack of attention and time to the interior. Yet the payoff of good work and attention to detail is quite satisfying.

This section begins with basic vacuuming and dusting, such as you would do with just a wash job. But then it goes on to examine the needs of each specific area of the interior: seats, carpets, doors, dash, etc. It focuses on deep cleaning, conditioning, and protecting. Most important, this section shows you the techniques that add up to a show-winning job.

VACUUMING AND DUSTING

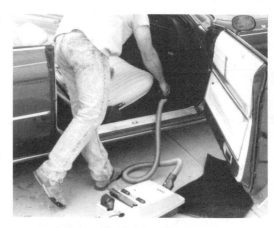

Remove the floor mats and vacuum the carpets. *Move the front seats to get at the carpet underneath.*

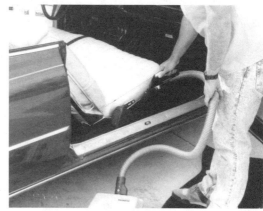

Use a crevice tool to get into tight spots, *such as around the seats, center console, and pedals.*

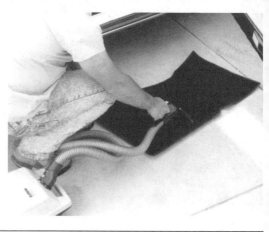

Vacuum or shake out the floor mats. *Vinyl mats should be washed and treated with protectant. Badly soiled carpet mats should be shampooed (page 118).*

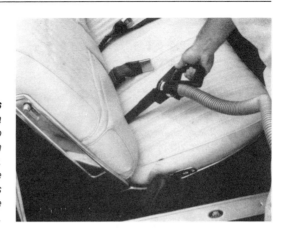

Vacuum the seats thoroughly. *Use a crevice tool to reach into seams and joints between the seats and backrest. On two-door vehicles, be sure to fold the front seats forward and vacuum the exposed area.*

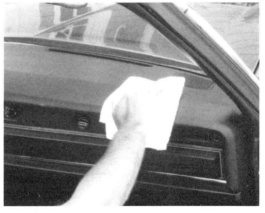

With a damp T-shirt rag, dust the dashboard and remove fingerprints from vinyl and hard surfaces. *A bit of spray-on all-purpose cleaner is useful for this purpose.*

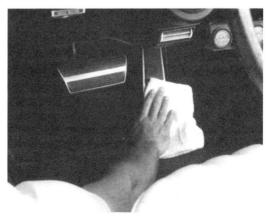

Install the floor mats, and clean the floor pedals and heel pads. *The following pages show how to proceed with interior detailing on different types of seats and trim.*

VINYL SEATS AND TRIM

The key to cleaning vinyl is to use vinyl upholstery shampoo and a small scrub brush. The brush is absolutely essential for deep cleaning. After scrubbing, wipe off the shampoo with a damp terry-cloth rag.

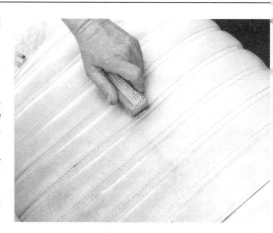

Look closely for dirt around metal trim. Here, we actually removed the metal panel to clean this area.

A real problem area is under folding seat backs. A toothbrush or stiff detailing brush with upholstery shampoo is needed for deep cleaning here.

This is more like it!
Back-seat passengers will be impressed with your diligence. Also, clean carefully around seat belt hardware and holders.

Use vinyl upholstery shampoo and a scrub brush on all vinyl trim throughout the interior: Door panels, kick panels under the dash, and sun visors.

Finish the job with a light coat of vinyl protectant. Be careful not to get the seats slippery. (We show door detailing on this same car on page 120.)

Detailing Cars & Trucks

FABRIC SEATS AND TRIM

Vacuum the interior thoroughly. *Remove floor mats, and shake them out, or vacuum them separately. Use a crevice tool to get in the tight spots around and under the seats and between the cushions.*

Pre-clean food and grease stains. *Treat spots with fabric upholstery shampoo, and scrub them with a brush. We prefer foaming aerosol shampoo because it is easy to use.*

Apply upholstery shampoo to all the fabric. *Thoroughly cover the fabric, but don't soak it, or it could take hours to dry and possibly create mildew.*

Deep clean dirty areas with a brush to remove embedded grime. *Wipe the fabric with a clean lint-free cloth, and allow it to dry.*

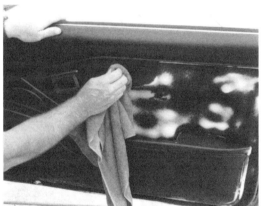

Clean other fabric trim, like door panels, with the same shampoo. *The dirt isn't likely to be as deeply embedded as it is on seats, so scrub with a towel rather than a brush to minimize "cleaning" wear of the fabric. Once the upholstery is dry, treat it with Scotchgard or similar fabric protectant.*

For heavy soil or stains, a steam cleaner may be necessary. *Quality units can be rented at supermarkets and hardware stores, or you can have the upholstery cleaned professionally when your household carpeting is shampooed.*

LEATHER SEATS AND TRIM

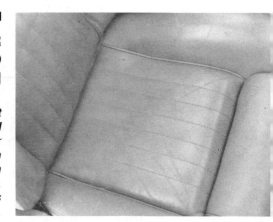

Typical leather seat problem: dirt-filled wrinkles. *This tan-color leather seat had been cleaned several times in the preceding months, but the dark wrinkles seemed permanent.*

Apply leather cleaner with a terry-cloth rag. *Use a generous amount of cleaner, and rub briskly.*

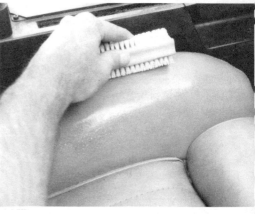

Here's the key: scrub seams, wrinkles, and all dirty surfaces with a stiff brush. *Using a brush is what really reaches down into the leather and lets the cleaner do its job.*

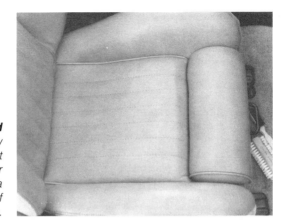

The freshly scrubbed leather seat. *Notice how the wrinkles have almost vanished because of our deep cleaning. This was a minor miracle, in view of previous failures.*

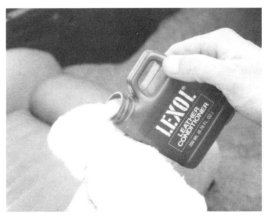

Apply leather conditioner with a fresh terry-cloth rag. *This product protects the leather, and restores life, suppleness, and sheen. Let it sit for about 10 minutes, and buff the seat with a dry towel.*

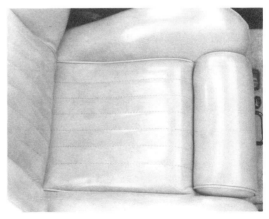

The finished seat. *Compare this with where we started. It looks a bit shiny in this photo, because we applied several coats of conditioner and snapped our shot. By the following day, the sheen was very correct.*

CARPET CLEANING

After a thorough vacuuming, spray foaming aerosol carpet cleaner on the entire carpet. This type of product is actually quite dry, and won't soak the carpet.

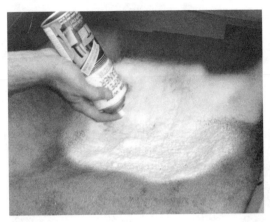

Scrub the carpet thoroughly, then let the foam dry. Be sure to use a nice stiff brush to get up the dirt. Drying may take several hours.

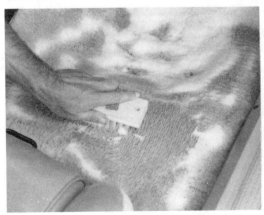

For stubborn spots, use an appropriate household carpet spot remover. Vigorously scrub the area with a brush, then a damp terry-cloth towel. Let it air dry.

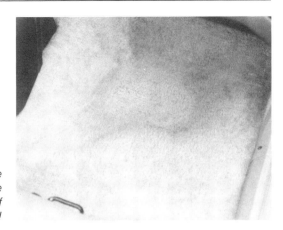

The finished carpet. *The stain is gone, and the carpet is a couple of shades lighter as well!*

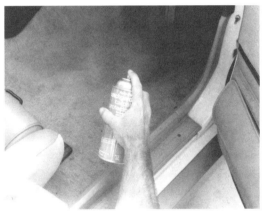

It's a good idea to spray the carpet with a protectant like Scotchgard. *This retards soiling and staining.*

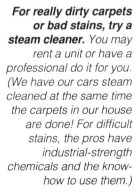

For really dirty carpets or bad stains, try a steam cleaner. *You may rent a unit or have a professional do it for you. (We have our cars steam cleaned at the same time the carpets in our house are done! For difficult stains, the pros have industrial-strength chemicals and the know-how to use them.)*

DOOR DETAILING

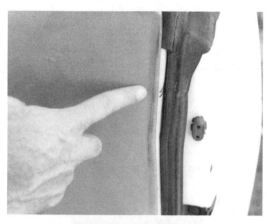

Residue from the rubber door molding has ground into this vinyl door panel. *Use vinyl cleaner and a nail brush to remove the grime.*

Clean the door edges with all-purpose cleaner, and remove old lube stickers. *Door edges collect a lot of dirt and are extremely visible, yet are often overlooked.*

Remove the stubborn adhesive left by old lube stickers. *WD-40 works quite well, as does automotive adhesive remover. (But, we bet you have a can of WD-40 around the garage.)*

Apply exterior rubber and vinyl protectant to weather stripping and plastic components. *Use a cotton rag to avoid overspray.*

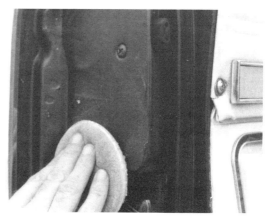

Protect the paint with a one-step cleaner-wax. *When it dries, buff it with a terry-cloth towel. Remove any residue with a toothbrush.*

A finished, shiny door edge. *We've put on a new maintenance sticker purchased at our local auto parts store.*

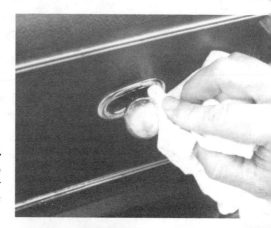

Clean and polish door handles and trim. *Use the appropriate chrome or plastic polish, as described in Section 6.*

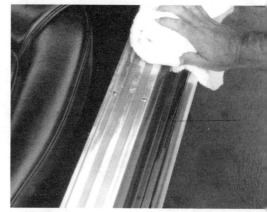

Clean and polish door sills. *Use appropriate aluminum, chrome, or plastic polish.*

Clean and detail door jambs. *Use the same techniques as shown on the preceding pages for door edges. If necessary, it's a good idea to lube hinges, strikers, and locks. (See the Do-It-Right Book "Lube, Oil, and Chassis Service" for details.)*

DASHBOARD DETAILING

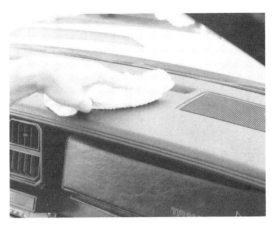

Clean the top of the dashboard and apply several coats of vinyl protectant, if appropriate. *Exposure to direct sunlight requires greater protection.*

Don't forget the edges of the dashboard. *This is an often overlooked spot!*

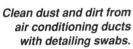

Clean dust and dirt from air conditioning ducts with detailing swabs. *These swabs are "audio tape head cleaners." Q-Tips also work, but leave a bit of lint. The important point is to get the ducts really clean.*

Open the vents and clean the visible surface inside the ducts. *It may take several swabs to do the job well. (If you're concerned about bacteria growth in air conditioning ducts, you might want to apply a bacteriostat from a hospital supply company.)*

Use a swab or Q-Tip to clean every crack and crevice where dirt can collect. *This is necessary attention to detailed cleaning that distinguishes a top-quality job.*

Clean gauge faces with plastic polish. *On older cars with glass gauge faces, use automotive window cleaner. Make sure each face is perfectly clean, with no fingerprints or haze.*

Clean the shifter boot and treat it with appropriate protectant. *It seems like this is a "dirt collector" on almost every vehicle we detail.*

Clean the steering wheel. *If it is vinyl or leather covered, use only a non-slippery protectant on it. Some exterior protectants can make the steering wheel slippery enough to make driving unsafe!*

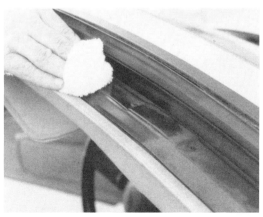

If installed: open and clean the sunroof. *Pay close attention to all the areas that are exposed only when it is open. These can get filthy, and yet are often overlooked in routine cleaning.*

Clean both sides of the visors. *Use appropriate shampoo and a towel for soiled areas.*

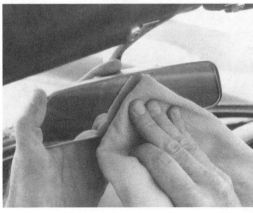

Clean the inside rear view mirror with window cleaner. *Scrub it good—it often has a build-up of dust and smoke residue.*

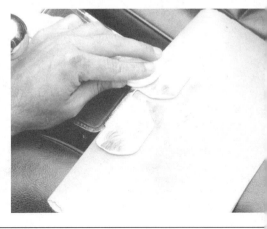

Clean chrome trim on the door and in the cockpit. *You may find it handy to use a piece of cardboard to protect adjacent surfaces.*

SEAT BELT CLEANING

Pull the seat belts all the way out of the retractor device. *Use a small pair of vise grips, or four clothespins to keep the belt fully extended.*

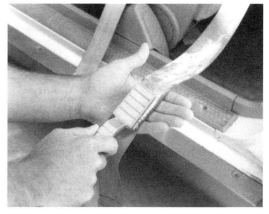

Scrub the belt with a mild wash solution. *We used car wash soap in warm water. Scrub the belts well on both sides to get them clean. Do NOT use any solvents or chemicals on your seatbelts, which could weaken them. Check your vehicle Owner's Manual for any specific precautions.*

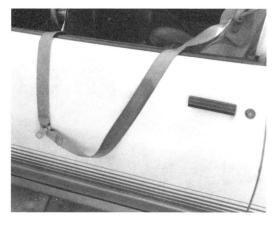

Wipe off the wash solution with a damp terry-cloth towel, and let the belts air dry. *A clean seat belt is another sign of careful detailing.*

TRUNK DETAILING

What a mess! Besides being filled with junk, the spare tire is not properly stowed in its well under the carpet. This trunk is a typical project.

Empty everything, and remove the carpet. You need a clear playing field to do a good job of trunk detailing. There's no special techniques in this job, but you must be thorough.

Vacuum the trunk interior and the carpet. The carpet is much easier to do when it's out of the trunk.

Clean the entire trunk with all-purpose cleaner. *Spray it everywhere, let it soak in, and clean it off with a terry-cloth towel. (You may apply a one-step cleaner-wax if you like.)*

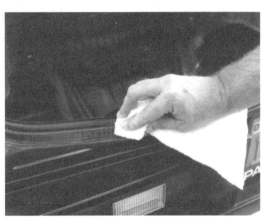

Apply exterior rubber and vinyl protectant. *Cover the trunk seal well, and don't forget the vinyl-covered panels inside the trunk.*

Properly stow the spare tire, jack, floor panel, and carpet. *Check the tire pressure in the spare. Make sure the securing hardware holds it and the jack securely in place. Big difference, huh?*

A FINAL TOUCH

If desired, spray a shot of deodorizer or air freshener in the interior. A pleasant scent is a nice final touch for your hard work!

Section 10:
Professional Underhood Detailing

The key to a successful engine detailing job is enhancing contrast. Contrast is easiest to see in the engine compartment of a new car or truck, where all the different colors, levels of gloss, and textures are still fresh.

The engine compartment of this Acura is a study in contrast—from the high-gloss black body color on the firewall to the matte black of the ignition shielding, from the shiny plated brackets to the as-cast aluminum of the fuel-injection plenum.

ENGINE CLEANING OPTIONS

There are three basic options for engine cleaning, depending on the degree of deterioration or neglect:

■ **Professional steam cleaning**—This is for a really filthy engine, one that's probably never been cleaned and has lots of thick grease and grime. Not only is this a tough job, but the resulting mess is too much for your yard—and your neighborhood. Be a responsible tenant of Planet Earth, and entrust this job to an automotive steam-cleaning service (check the Yellow Pages). If you'll be doing your own detailing, tell them; many steam-cleaning services also detail engines, so make sure you both agree on who's doing what.

■ **Self-serve car-wash cleaning**—A self-serve car wash is a great way to clean a moderately dirty and *oily* engine compartment. They use hot water and high pressure. Protect the carburetor and distributor as described in this section. Wear eye protection, and don't direct the hot water at information stickers, fuse panels, the alternator, or other electrical components. We get the worst grime off at the car wash and then do the detail cleaning shown here at home.

■ **Driveway chemical cleaning**—This is the job we show you here in this section— using a spray-on chemical solvent and a hose to wash it off. This procedure works well unless the engine is really grimy. We use it as a final step after a steam-cleaning or car-wash hot-water cleaning to ensure the engine is scrupulously clean before detailing.

DRIVEWAY ENGINE WASHING

For an engine compartment that's cleaned at least once a year, all that's needed is a thorough cleaning with solvent, followed with a soap-and-water wash, and a good rinse. You will need engine cleaning solvent (page 22), dish-washing detergent or all-purpose cleaner, engine-cleaning brushes, and clean rags and paper towels. For comfort and safety, we recommend you perform this procedure with the engine cool. Our project engine here is a 1968 Chevelle big block.

Remove the air cleaner, and protect the carburetor and distributor with plastic bags. Tape them securely in place so they will keep dirt and water out of the engine while it's being washed and rinsed.

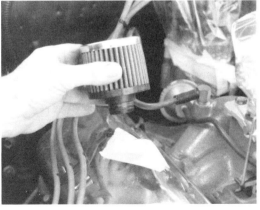

Remove foam- or paper-element breathers, and cover the holes with tape to keep dirt and water out of the engine.

Spray chemical cleaner on the engine, and loosen stubborn deposits with a stiff brush. *Apply the cleaner generously wherever you find heavy deposits. Wear eye protection against splashback for all of the scrubbing and rinsing steps.*

Use a toothbrush to get into tight spots. *Remove deposits along mating surfaces, such as where manifolds bolt to the cylinder head and block. Dirt left in these places is a telltale sign of a poor job.*

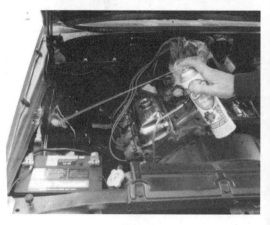

Spray chemical cleaner on the firewall, inner fenders, and frame. *These areas collect grime at about the same rate as the engine.*

Thoroughly rinse the engine and entire engine compartment with clear water. *Pay particular attention to nooks and crannies. Avoid spraying directly at the carburetor, distributor, and taped-over openings.*

Rinse the outside of the vehicle. *Flush off all dirt and solvent film from the fenders, cowl, and windshield.*

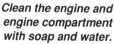

Clean the engine and engine compartment with soap and water. *Wash everything, including the firewall, inner fenders, accessories, hoses, radiator, and the engine. Then flush with fresh water to remove dirt, solvent film, and soap suds.*

Dry the engine and the engine compartment. *Use old towels to wipe off the bulk of the water.*

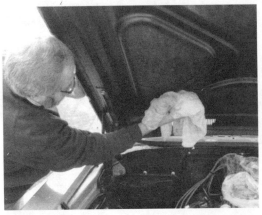

Don't forget the underside of the hood. *Not only will water continue to drip on the engine if you don't dry the hood, but the hood itself should be as clean as the rest of the engine compartment.*

Remove the plastic from the carburetor and distributor. *Make sure that no water puddled on the plastic gets into either component.*

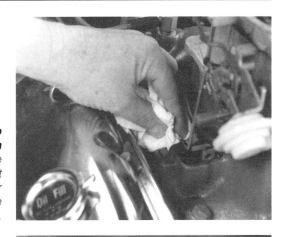

Use paper towels to soak up water trapped in pockets. *Don't leave water on the engine, or it will dry and form water spots when the engine gets hot.*

Dry the distributor cap, spark plug wires, boots, and spark plugs. *Even when it's protected, the distributor may be damp inside.*

With the engine really clean, you can see some very nice enhancement of the contrast of colors and textures in the engine compartment. Now you're ready to begin the serious—and fun—part of engine detailing: touch-up painting (as needed), polishing, and protecting.

ENGINE PAINTING

Original engine colors are available for virtually all vehicles. *Also, black paint, in both gloss and semi-gloss is commonly available.*

These four spray finishes handle the details in most underhood jobs. *Silver metallic simulates cadmium plating. Clear retards rust and corrosion formation on unprotected parts with a "natural" appearance. Semi-flat black and gloss black are used to touch up chips and wear on appropriately painted items.*

Using tape and aluminum foil, mask complicated parts, hard lines, and wiring to protect them from paint overspray. *Wrap the foil loosely around the things you want to protect.*

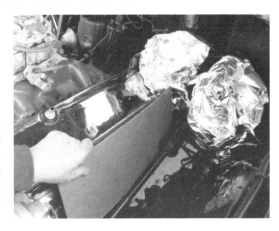

A cardboard paint block is useful for temporarily masking areas while you paint. Just hold the paint block in front of the area you want to protect as you spray.

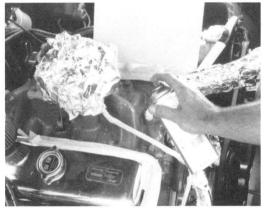

Apply several light coats of engine paint rather than a single heavy coat. Allow the paint to dry between coats to minimize runs.

Remove all foil and masking tape. Enjoy a fresh-looking engine!

POLISHING &
PROTECTING

Use a one-step cleaner-wax or plastic polish on glossy surfaces, like this inner panel. Engine compartment enamel is usually softer than exterior paint, so don't use heavy-duty abrasive cleaners.

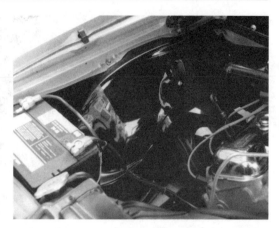

Polish and wax the air cleaner before reinstalling it. The air cleaner is one of the first things noticed when the hood is opened.

Use exterior rubber and vinyl (ERV) protectant on plastic and low-gloss paint surfaces. Burnish the surface with a dry towel to get rid of excess and smooth the gloss.

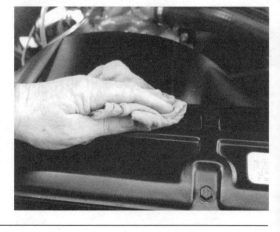

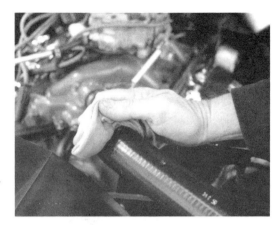

Use ERV protectant on hoses, wiring, and soft parts. *Burnish the protectant after it dries.*

Clean all underhood chrome with chrome or metal polish. *Then protect with carnauba wax.*

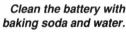

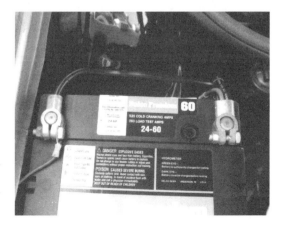

Clean the battery with baking soda and water. *This effectively cuts corrosion around the terminals. (For the complete story on cleaning and servicing your battery, see the "Tune-Up and Electrical Service" book in the Do-It-Right Professional Tips & Techniques series.)*

SOME EXTRA-SPECIAL TOUCHES

Engine detailing reaches a point where it borders on restoration work. This is when the engine compartment no longer just looks clean and tidy but begins to look new. If you are a really particular owner, here are some extra-special touches for your detailing job. Most of these tasks involve additional painting and the replacement of hardware and parts.

Aluminum and dull-plated parts, like the cap on this power steering fluid reservoir, can be touched up with silver or aluminum spray paint. Thoroughly clean and dry the part before painting, and use wax-and-silicone remover to ensure a good finish.

High-temperature stainless-steel paint* makes exhaust manifolds look brand new—and keeps them that way. Remove all dirt and rust and brush the paint on. This manifold was refinished nearly a year ago and looks like it just came from the foundry!

(*Available from the Eastwood Company 1-800-345-1178.)

When practical, parts like this alternator bracket should be removed, cleaned, and painted. When this isn't practical, a satisfactory touch-up job can be done with a brush and paint of the correct color and gloss level.

This master cylinder and windshield wiper motor look pretty drab. Even when clean, deteriorated parts like these can detract from a first-rate engine detailing. But with a little help . . .

. . . They look new! The wiper motor was finished with silver spray paint, and the master cylinder has been painted with Eastwood's Spray Gray cast-iron finish. The irridited master cylinder cap was cleaned with a chemical chrome cleaner so the soft irridite plating wasn't removed.

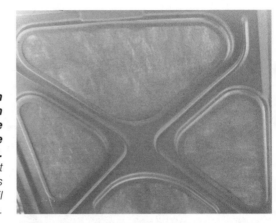

Greasy or torn underhood insulation can spoil the appearance of the engine compartment. Fresh replacement insulation like this adds yet another correct detail to the job.

New, plated hardware is inexpensive and adds a bright touch to your engine detailing job. When replacing bolts such as those for the hood hinges, replace them one at a time so the hood remains in alignment.

Here are the results of several hours of satisfying engine detailing work. Damaged and missing heater and vacuum hoses have been replaced. This may look like restoration work, but the engine in this 23-year-old car is maintained at this level!

Section 11:

Truck Chassis Detailing

INTRODUCTION

Detailing a truck requires no procedures or products that are different from those we have already shown you in this book. Paint is paint, chrome is chrome. However, the *focus* of truck detailing—particularly 4x4's—can include quite a bit more time and attention on the chassis. Not only does *more* of the chassis show, but due to the weekend duties of many of these warriors, they can get their undersides a bit soiled.

Our goal in this section is to show you two detailing projects on real-world driving-and-hauling 4x4's—not show trucks. What we do here is representative of what you can do to make your truck look great.

Good suspension and chassis detailing uses the same techniques of cleaning, painting, polishing, and protecting that we showed you in the previous section on engine detailing. Here, however, you'll be doing a lot of the work on your knees and on your back. (Be sure to wear goggles.) The goals are also the same: (1) get rid of the dirt and grime with thorough degreasing and washing, and (2) restore original colors and shine with paint and polish.

BLAZER PROJECT

Our first detailing project is a 5-year old Blazer. It has a lot of off-the-shelf chrome parts in its custom high-riding chassis. As well as providing daily transportation, this truck sees regular weekend off-road work on the deserts of Southern California. A point you should note is that the owner washes and cleans this undercarriage after every off-road trip. Our beginning point was a clean chassis. Note well that one of the most beneficial things you can do for your truck is to clean it regularly.

The Blazer's front axle shows minor dirt buildup, chipped paint, and light rust on exposed metal. This is a good beginning point for detailing. (If your chassis is filthy and greasy, it should be professionally steam cleaned, as discussed on page 132.)

Clean the suspension to remove dirt and grease. *An all-purpose cleaner such as Simple Green works well for a job like this one. Use a scrub brush and a toothbrush to get out all the dirt and grease.*

Clean gold irridite-plated parts with a liberal amount of chrome cleaner and a soft toothbrush. *Don't use pressure to clean this type of plating, or you will wear it off.*

Thoroughly clean all chrome with a chrome or metal polish. *Then protect it with wax, just like you would exterior chrome trim.*

Use aluminum foil to protect chrome and other parts you don't want painted or oversprayed. Use masking tape where appropriate.

Also use cardboard or newspaper to prevent overspray. Here, we're protecting the brake and the inside of the wheel while touching up this steering knuckle.

The renewed contrast of bright, clean chrome against deep satiny black was achieved with less than an hour's work on the front suspension of this 4x4. The simpler rear suspension takes even less time.

FORD TRUCK PROJECT

The 3/4-ton Ford truck used in this project is only two years old. It is virtually stock except for off-road tires, chrome wheels, and multiple shock absorbers. While it is used as a daily driver and an occasional off-roader, we must again make the point that the owner takes good care of the underside—with frequent washing and scrubbing. So our starting point here is truly launching into detailing specifics.

The result of regular cleaning of wheel wells and underbody—this area reflects pride of ownership and a respect for the investment involved. The only deterioration is the beginning of rust on bolts and rivet heads.

We touched up the rivet heads with low-gloss black spray paint. We used a cardboard paint block to prevent overspray.

We chose to protect the inner fenders, splash shields, and frame with ERV protectant rather than polish and wax. The protectant deepens the finish on these painted and plastic areas, helps them shed water and mud, and doesn't remove the soft paint as polish would.

Treat shock boots with ERV protectant. This keeps them looking fresh and new, and also lengthens their life.

Treat chrome-plated parts with polish, followed by a coat of wax. The protection afforded by the wax is at least as important here, under the truck, as it is on bumpers and exterior trim.

Spray ERV protectant directly onto the tires.
The aggressive tread patterns on most off-road truck tires make it difficult to adequately cover the rubber with an applicator.

Burnish the protectant into the tires. This helps the protectant penetrate the surface of the tire and avoids a sloppy "painted-on" look.

Clean the wheels as described in Section 8.
Using the wrong cleaner can damage certain types of wheels. Wax the wheels to protect them and retard rust or corrosion.

Here are the results of an hour spent detailing wheels . . .

. . . Front wheel wells . . .

. . . And rear wheel wells and frame.

Section 12:

The 15-Minute Quick Wash

For those times when you have some special occasion that requires a clean car but no time to do the type of thorough job described in Section 3, you may find our "15-minute quick wash" exactly what you need.

The key to the quick wash is two wash mitts—one for each hand. Of course, you must move quickly to do the job in 15 minutes. We have timed this job with a stopwatch, and our 15-minute claim is *no* exaggeration! (We also timed two workers at a professional car wash which uses a two-mitt hand-wash technique. They could do a full wash—excluding the rinse off—in 60 to 90 seconds!) You'll need the wash kit described in Section 2. Be sure to park in the shade, because you will wash the whole car at one time.

FAST WASH

Rinse the whole car. *Get off as much dirt and dust as possible.*

Immediately begin washing at the top. *Don't let the car start to dry. Work your way down the windshield. Work quickly— the goal is to finish all soap washing in 5 minutes.*

Wash the entire car very quickly with both hands. *Use lots of soapy solution. Since you are not washing in sections, you MUST work quickly—so the soap doesn't dry on the car.*

Scrub each of the tires and wheels with your tire brush. *Move quickly from wheel to wheel.*

Rinse the whole car in one quick pass. *Make sure you get all the soap out of vents and cracks. Do the windows well.*

FAST DRY

Make a first drying pass with your chamois. *Don't worry about water streaks, the next pass will get them.*

Make a second drying pass with a terry-cloth towel. Catch the little drips and streaks on this run. Give the windows and mirrors a thorough drying, since you won't have time for glass cleaner in this quick wash.

FAST FINISH

Quick-dust the interior with a damp towel. Wipe the top of the dash, door panels, ornaments—the dusty places.

Apply exterior rubber and vinyl protectant to the tires. Start at the center and work your way outward. You should have time for this in our 15-minute budget, and the results are worth it. Put away your kit and you're done. Pant... Pant...!

Section 13:
Time Saver: One-Step Cleaner-Wax Job

One-step products which clean, polish, and wax all at the same time can't give you the same results as the three-step process shown in Section 5. But, when you don't have time for the full multi-step job, the one-steps really shine—if you'll excuse the pun! When correctly applied, a one-step cleaner-wax will yield excellent results in both shine and protection. They are so good, in fact, that many people are completely satisfied to go no farther with paint cleaning and detailing. And we know of some fussy types who use one-steps to keep their cars looking good between major detailing sessions. Like everything else we've talked about in this book, good results come from correct application.

APPLYING ONE-STEP CLEANER-WAX

Load your foam pad with one-step cleaner-wax. *If you're using a liquid product, pour a small amount on the pad.*

Apply the cleaner-wax to an area of a few square feet. *Here it was about half the hood.*

Rub the cleaner-wax into the finish in one direction. *This is where the cleaning chemicals remove oxidation and grime. It is normal to see the pad get quite black and/or paint colored.*

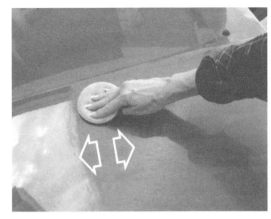

Next, continue rubbing the cleaner-wax perpendicular to the first direction. *Continue using moderate pressure to deep-clean the paint.*

Finally, rub the cleaner-wax in a circular motion. *This "three-direction" procedure simply assures that you've cleaned the paint thoroughly and distributed the wax evenly. Be sure to get into all the edges and tight spots.*

Move on to the next section and continue rubbing in cleaner-wax. *With most products you can go ahead and cover the entire vehicle. (We've done half the hood here for photographic purposes.)*

PRO TIP: Apply Cleaner-Wax Wet or Dry?

Some one-step products suggest that you slightly wet the applicator before putting wax on the vehicle. This provides lubrication to make it easier to apply and to make the application more even. Other one-step products warn against using any moisture at all, so make sure you read the label.

For those products that can be used wet, it's better to moisten the surface rather than the applicator. This gives you better control over the amount of water so you're not likely to soak the applicator and dilute the cleaner so much that it fails to do its job.

Use a spray bottle to apply water to the paint. The bottle works much better than wetting the applicator itself.

Allow the cleaner-wax to dry and "cloud." This should take 10 to 15 minutes. The clouding signals that the wax is ready to buff.

BUFFING
ONE-STEP
CLEANER-WAX

Fold a clean T-shirt into a buffing "block" slightly larger than your hand. *A terry-cloth towel also works well.*

Buff off the cleaner residue with a circular motion. *Use moderate hand pressure to bring out the shine of the wax. Turn your buffing cloth over frequently to keep it from clogging with oxidation and dirt.*

Use a dry paint brush or detailing brush to clean all residue from cracks and crevices. *See page 73 for details on how to do this.*

The finished job! The car sparkles. *This was an author's wife's very first experience at car detailing, and she was delighted with the results.*

FINISHING TOUCHES

Only the paint detailing goes faster with a one-step cleaner-wax. You still need to detail the trim as shown in Section 6, the tires and wheels as shown in Section 8, and the interior as shown in Section 9.

INDEX

A

Air conditioning ducts, detailing of 123-124

Air freshener 130

All-purpose wheel cleaner 19, 96-97, 102

Aluminum and magnesium wheel cleaner 19, 98

B

Bacteriostat 124

Battery detailing 141

Brushes

Pro Tip on using to remove wax residue 73-74

Types used in detailing 23

Buffer, see Electric orbital buffer

Bug and tar remover, see Tar and bug remover

C

Carnauba wax

Applicator 24

Purpose 13

Pro Tip on potential problems with polymer sealants 16

Pro Tip on removing wax residue 73-74

Products available 16

See also One-step cleaner-wax, Paint waxing or Paint detailing

Carpet cleaner and shampoo 20, 118

Carpet cleaning, see Interior detailing

Chamois

Pro Tip on choosing 11

Used for drying 39, 40, 49

Chrome and metal polish 21, 76, 78, 98, 99, 101, 103, 105, 141, 147

Chrome and wire wheel cleaner 19, 100-101, 104

Chrome trim, see Trim detailing

Cleaner

Carpet, see Carpet cleaner and shampoo

Engine, See Engine cleaner

Glass, See Glass cleaner

Leather, see Leather cleaner and conditioner

Paint, see Paint cleaning or Paint detailing

Upholstery, see Upholstery cleaner and shampoo

Wheel, see Wheel cleaner

Cleaner-wax, see One-step cleaner-wax

Clear-coat paint

One-step cleaner-wax for 17

Paint cleaner for 14

See also Paint detailing

Compound, products available 18

Conditioner, see Leather conditioner

Conventional paint

One-step cleaner-wax for 17

Paint cleaner for 14

See also Paint detailing

SHOPPING LIST

Washing Products and Tools
- ❑ Tar & bug remover
- ❑ Car-wash soap
- ❑ All-purpose cleaner
- ❑ Automotive glass cleaner
- ❑ Bucket (2 for no-hose wash)
- ❑ Wash mitt (2 for fast wash or 2-bucket wash)
- ❑ Hose
- ❑ Spring-loaded hose nozzle
- ❑ Tire brush
- ❑ Chamois
- ❑ Cotton terry-cloth towels

Paint Detailing Products

Show-Quality Products (3 steps):
- ❑ Paint cleaner (deoxidizer)
    - ❑ Clear-coat ❑ Conventional

    Oxidation is
    ❑ Light ❑ Medium ❑ Heavy
- ❑ Paint polish or "glaze"
    - ❑ Normal ❑ Ultrafine
- ❑ Carnauba wax (no cleaner or polish)

Time-Saving Products:
(2-step or 1-step)
- ❑ Cleaner-polish (no wax)
    - ❑ Clear-coat ❑ Conventional
- ❑ Carnauba wax (no cleaner or polish)
- ❑ One-step cleaner-wax
    - ❑ Clear-coat ❑ Conventional

Wheel Cleaner
- ❑ All-purpose
- ❑ Chrome & wire wheel
- ❑ Polished or anodized aluminum
- ❑ Bare aluminum or magnesium

Tire Detailing Products
- ❑ Tire cleaner
- ❑ Rubber & vinyl protectant

Wheel & Trim Polish
- ❑ Chrome and metal polish
- ❑ Plastic polish

Interior & Vinyl-top Detailing Products
- ❑ Upholstery/top shampoo
    - ❑ Fabric ❑ Vinyl
- ❑ Carpet shampoo
- ❑ Leather cleaner
- ❑ Leather conditioner

Additional Detailing Products
- ❑ Engine degreaser
- ❑ Engine touch-up paint
- ❑ Accessory and chassis touch-up paint

Detailing Tools
- ❑ Wax applicator pad
- ❑ Toothbrush, detail brushes
- ❑ Scrub brushes
- ❑ Swabs
- ❑ Terry cloth towels (6 minimum)
- ❑ Clean T-shirt rags
- ❑ Window towels (lint-free cotton)
- ❑ Small dust pan and whisk broom
- ❑ Household vacuum cleaner
- ❑ Liquid applicator

Optional:
- ❑ Electric orbital buffer
- ❑ Spare bonnets

SHOPPING LIST

Washing Products and Tools
- ❏ Tar & bug remover
- ❏ Car-wash soap
- ❏ All-purpose cleaner
- ❏ Automotive glass cleaner
- ❏ Bucket (2 for no-hose wash)
- ❏ Wash mitt (2 for fast wash or 2-bucket wash)
- ❏ Hose
- ❏ Spring-loaded hose nozzle
- ❏ Tire brush
- ❏ Chamois
- ❏ Cotton terry-cloth towels

Paint Detailing Products

Show-Quality Products (3 steps):
- ❏ Paint cleaner (deoxidizer)
  - ❏ Clear-coat ❏ Conventional

  Oxidation is
  - ❏ Light ❏ Medium ❏ Heavy
- ❏ Paint polish or "glaze"
  - ❏ Normal ❏ Ultrafine
- ❏ Carnauba wax (no cleaner or polish)

Time-Saving Products: (2-step or 1-step)
- ❏ Cleaner-polish (no wax)
  - ❏ Clear-coat ❏ Conventional
- ❏ Carnauba wax (no cleaner or polish)
- ❏ One-step cleaner-wax
  - ❏ Clear-coat ❏ Conventional

Wheel Cleaner
- ❏ All-purpose
- ❏ Chrome & wire wheel
- ❏ Polished or anodized aluminum
- ❏ Bare aluminum or magnesium

Tire Detailing Products
- ❏ Tire cleaner
- ❏ Rubber & vinyl protectant

Wheel & Trim Polish
- ❏ Chrome and metal polish
- ❏ Plastic polish

Interior & Vinyl-top Detailing Products
- ❏ Upholstery/top shampoo
  - ❏ Fabric ❏ Vinyl
- ❏ Carpet shampoo
- ❏ Leather cleaner
- ❏ Leather conditioner

Additional Detailing Products
- ❏ Engine degreaser
- ❏ Engine touch-up paint
- ❏ Accessory and chassis touch-up paint

Detailing Tools
- ❏ Wax applicator pad
- ❏ Toothbrush, detail brushes
- ❏ Scrub brushes
- ❏ Swabs
- ❏ Terry cloth towels (6 minimum)
- ❏ Clean T-shirt rags
- ❏ Window towels (lint-free cotton)
- ❏ Small dust pan and whisk broom
- ❏ Household vacuum cleaner
- ❏ Liquid applicator

Optional:
- ❏ Electric orbital buffer
- ❏ Spare bonnets

COLOPHON

As well as being automotive enthusiasts, we are also quality book enthusiasts. The word colophon is from the Greek kolophon, meaning "summit, or finishing touch." We include one in this book because we know that many of you are interested in such things. Besides, this is a bit of tradition that we wish to perpetuate!

Type: The Helvetica family was chosen because of its excellent legibility and friendly appearance. The body type of this book is 10/12 Helvetica. Photo and illustration captions are 9/11 Helvetica-Bold and -Light. Captions are in Helvetica Black.

Photos: To eliminate harsh shadows, indoor shots were done with indirect umbrella lighting, and outdoor shots were done in open north-facing shade. Wherever possible, we show the reader's point of view and very close detail. Film developing and printing was done by The Darkroom, a professional lab in Northridge, California.

Illustrations: Illustrations were drawn from photo reference to ensure accuracy. We chose to include Mr. Amos' hand lettering because of its warmth and clarity.

Electronic page production: Manuscripts were prepared and edited in XyWrite on a 386 PC. Illustrations were scanned on a Microtek 300Z. Page layout, illustration sizing and cropping, and all typesetting was done on a 386 PC with Ventura 3.0 for Windows. Other important software used in the production of this book included Corel Draw 2.0, Adobe ATM 1.0, the Adobe Type Library, and of course, Windows 3.0. Page proofs were "pulled" on an NEC890 Postscript laser printer, and final camera-ready output was done on a Linotronic 300 by Flying Color Graphics in Canoga Park, California.

Printing and binding: Performed by Griffin Printing, a unique environmentally sensitive, employee-owned company in Glendale, California. Photos were prepared as 120-line halftone negatives and were hand-stripped. The body of the book was printed on 50-pound offset paper on a Timson full-web heat-set press. Covers were printed on a four-color Heidelberg press and were UV coated for resistance to soiling.

OTHER BOOKS IN THIS SERIES

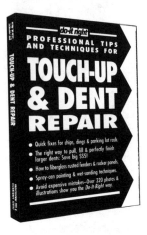

This book shows you how to do the easier types of body work and painting, from touch-up of minor chips and parking lot rash, to pulling and filling larger dents.

192 pages, 338 illustations
ISBN 1-879110-18-0

CONTENTS: 1 Introduction: • How to match your paint color • Where to find your vehicle's color code • Checking for frame misalignment **2 Tools and Supplies:** • For dent repairs • For fiberglass, ABS plastic, and rust-hole repairs • For dent pulling and metal working • For painting **3 How to Touch Up Minor Chips and Scratches:** • Surface preparation • How to fill paint chips • How to paint and wet-sand a small scratch **4 How to Fill Small Dings and Dents:** • How to prepare the dent surface for plastic body filler • How to mix and apply body filler • How to sand and finish body filler **5 Professional Dent Pulling Techniques:** • How to use a suction-cup puller on "oil-can" dents • How to use a T-handle puller on small dents • How to map and drill a dent for slide-hammer pulling • How to use a slide-hammer puller **6 A Larger Dent-Pulling Project:** • Mapping and pulling • Applying body filler • How to use a disk sander • Shaping and sanding • Surface preparation • Final finish **7 Hammer and Dolly Techniques:** • Planning your approach • How to hammer on-dolly • How to hammer off-dolly • How to perform fine hammering **8 How to Repair Cracks in Fiberglass and ABS:** • How to prepare yourself for working with fiberglass • How to stop cracks in progress • How to prepare the surface • How to mix resin and apply the patch • Final finish **9 How to Permanently Repair Minor Rust Holes and Damage:** • How to prepare the sheet metal • How to prepare and apply patches • Fiberglass tips and shortcuts that don't work • Final finish **10 How to Paint Small Areas with a Spray Can:** • Finish sanding • Soft-edge technique for masking • Aerosol spray painting technique • How to apply primer • How to apply color and clear-coat paint • How to use an airbrush for touch-up • How to wet-sand and polish new paint for maximum gloss • How to use a paint block.

TUNE-UP CONTENTS: 1 Tune-Up Overview:
• The correct steps and sequence for a tune-up
• Tuning a modern electronic engine **2 Tune-Up Parts, Supplies and Tools:** • Examination of what you need **3 Valve Adjustment:** • How mechanical and hydraulic valve lifters work • How to fix noisy lifters **4 Compression Test:** • How to perform dry and wet compression tests • How to interpret test results **5 Spark Plugs:** • Reading engine condition • How to know if you need hotter or colder spark plugs • How to prepare and install new plugs **6 Distributor and Wires:** • How to test spark plug wires • How to assemble "universal" wire kits • How to install new ignition wires • How to inspect, test, and service the distributor • How to use a tach/dwell meter • How to check and adjust ignition timing **7 Carburetor/Fuel Injection:** • How to clean a carburetor • How to clean and inspect a fuel-injection system • How to replace the fuel filter(s) • How to inspect and test a PCV system • How to replace the air filter • How to adjust idle speed • Oldies only—fast-idle and mixture adjustment.

ELECTRICAL SERVICE CONTENTS:
8 Electrical Parts, Supplies and Tools: • A look at what you need **9 Battery:** • How a battery works and what can go wrong • How to inspect and service the battery • How to test condition with a hydrometer • How to select and replace • How to charge • How to measure and replace battery cables **10 Lamps and Wiring:** • How to replace sealed-beam and quartz-halogen headlamps • How to upgrade tungsten headlamps to quartz-halogen • How to aim headlamps • How to replace exterior and interior lamp bulbs • How to troubleshoot bulb burnout problems • How to replace damaged wires and sockets **11 Fuses and Circuit Breakers:** • How to inspect and replace fuses and fusible links • How to install an in-line fuse holder **12 Charging System:** • How to troubleshoot problems in the alternator and charging system • How to replace the alternator **13 Starting System:** • How to troubleshoot starter problems • How to replace the starter.

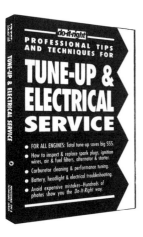

This is a complete guide to two types of important DIY jobs.
Part A, Tune-Up, gives you a 5-step procedure for inspecting and tuning virtually any gasoline engine. Part B, Electrical Service, shows you how to perform a number of easy, money-saving electrical jobs.

192 pages, 219 illustrations
ISBN 1-879110-15-6

LUBRICATION CONTENTS: 1 Save Money with Frequent Maintenance: • Why more frequent maintenance costs less • How to keep you vehicle under warranty with DIY work **2 Parts, Supplies, and Tools:** • The rundown on what you need **3 Engine Oil and Filter Change:** • How to select the best oil and additives • Is synthetic oil right for your engine? • How to read oil condition • How to change oil and filter correctly **4 Steering and Suspension:** • How to install permanent grease fittings • How to lube steering and suspension • How to inspect for bushing wear • How to replace constant-velocity (CV) joint boots • How to check springs and torsion bars **5 Transmission and Drivetrain:** • How to change manual transmission oil • How to interpret fluid condition • How to change automatic transmission fluid and screen "leak-free" • How to inspect and change differential oil • How to lube driveshaft slip joints • How to service front wheel bearings **6 Four-Wheel Drive:** • How to change differential oil • How to change transfer case oil • How to lube slip joints and front-axle CV-joints

CHASSIS MAINTENANCE CONTENTS: 7 Drive Belts: • How to inspect and adjust • How to select the correct type • How to replace • How to put together a "free" emergency belt kit **8 Cooling System:** • Complete cooling system "tune-up" • How to test coolant freeze-protection capability • How to install a permanent coolant flushing fitting • How to reverse-flush the cooling system • How to inspect and replace radiator and heater hoses • How to replace the thermostat **9 Brake System:** • How to check and replenish brake fluid • How to inspect disk brake pads and rotor • How to fix squealing disk brakes • How to inspect and replace brake fluid • How to bleed a brake system • How to flush and replace the fluid **10 Shock Absorbers:** • How to test shock and strut condition • How to select and replace • Understanding mountings **11 Exhaust System:** • How to inspect the complete exhaust system **12 Body:** • How to lubricate body hinges and latches • How to select and replace wipers.

This book gives you instructions for a complete professional lubrication service. It also includes instruction for a number of important chassis maintenance and repair jobs. There is a chapter on special considerations for 4-wheel-drive vehicles.

192 pages, 236 illustrations
ISBN 1-879110-16-4

ORDER FORM & INFORMATION REQUEST

We recommend you purchase Do-It-Right books from your local retailer, where you purchased this book. But if you would like to order from us or add your name to our mailing list for future product announcements, please use this form.

Name: _____

Mail to:
Do-It-Right Publishing
147 East Holly Street, Suite 304
Pasadena, CA 91103

Credit card orders, call toll-free:

1-800-223-3556

10-5 Pacific Time, Monday-Friday

Address: _____

_____

City: _____ State: _____ Zip: _____

Daytime phone: _____
(in case we have to call about this order)

Title	Price Each	Quantity	Total
Tune-Up & Electrical Service	$8.95		
Lube, Oil & Chassis Service	$8.95		
Detailing Cars & Trucks	$8.95		
Touch-Up & Dent Repair	$8.95		
Total book order			
California residents: 6.5% tax (58¢ per book)			
Shipping & handling per order			$1.95
TOTAL AMOUNT			

Paid by: ❑ Check ❑ Master Charge ❑ Visa ❑ American Express

Make checks payable to **Do-It-Right**.

Account No:_____ Expiration date: _____

Your Signature: _____

Orders are shipped immediately. Please allow several weeks for delivery.

❑ Please add me to your mailing list for new book and video announcements.

❑ Please send me a brochure on your model-specific factory-approved DIY manuals and shop manuals for: ❑ Nissan vehicles ❑ Hyundai vehicles.

Over for your comments.

Your comments on this *Detailing Cars & Trucks* manual
would be appreciated.

_____

_____

_____

_____

I rate this book
❏ Excellent ❏ Very Good ❏ OK ❏ Poor

Other titles I would like to see from Do-It-Right:

_____ ❏ Book ❏ Video

_____ ❏ Book ❏ Video

FOLD HERE AND STAPLE OR TAPE SHUT

_____

_____

_____

| PLACE |
| STAMP |
| HERE |

Do-It-Right Publishing
147 East Holly Street, Suite 304
Pasadena, CA 91103

Do-It-Right Books are Different. Here is Why.

"After training factory technicians for 18 years, we wanted to bring the same type of concise job-specific training to DIYer's. This Professional Tips and Techniques Series is the result. We hope you enjoy it."

Photos and Illustrations Tell the Story. We believe that automotive instruction should be as *visual* as possible, because do-it-yourself work is a visual, hands-on process. We begin every book with a storyboard plan and a camera full of film. Our goal is to *show* you rather than to *tell* you how to do each job.

We Focus on Real-World Money-Saving Jobs. In our judgment, each job must (1) be easy for a DIYer to do with ordinary tools and skills, (2) have low risk of failure, and (3) be a meaningful money-saver. We assume that your prime motivation for DIY work is to save money!

Each Book is a Mini-Course. While certainly nothing like a school textbook, each book in this *Professional Tips and Techniques Series* provides an in-depth treatment of the jobs it covers. Each book builds your automotive knowledge and hands-on skills. Each book prepares you to attempt new tasks and produce quality results.

A "Good Read!" We are automotive enthusiasts, and we've tried to share that love with you! We've included a lot of background info on *why* jobs are done a certain way, rather than just giving you procedures to follow blindly. We've openly shared our opinions. And we've worked hard to bring you condensed, up-to-date, and interesting information for DIY work in the 90's.

If you would like to be notified of future Do-It-Right books and videos, please send us your name and address on the enclosed form. We welcome your suggestions and comments to help us improve our books.

Dennis Holmes

SHOPPING LIST

Washing Products and Tools
- ❏ Tar & bug remover
- ❏ Car-wash soap
- ❏ All-purpose cleaner
- ❏ Automotive glass cleaner
- ❏ Bucket (2 for no-hose wash)
- ❏ Wash mitt (2 for fast wash or 2-bucket wash)
- ❏ Hose
- ❏ Spring-loaded hose nozzle
- ❏ Tire brush
- ❏ Chamois
- ❏ Cotton terry-cloth towels

Paint Detailing Products
Show-Quality Products (3 steps):
- ❏ Paint cleaner (deoxidizer)
    - ❏ Clear-coat ❏ Conventional
    - Oxidation is
    - ❏ Light ❏ Medium ❏ Heavy
- ❏ Paint polish or "glaze"
    - ❏ Normal ❏ Ultrafine
- ❏ Carnauba wax (no cleaner or polish)

Time-Saving Products: (2-step or 1-step)
- ❏ Cleaner-polish (no wax)
    - ❏ Clear-coat ❏ Conventional
- ❏ Carnauba wax (no cleaner or polish)
- ❏ One-step cleaner-wax
    - ❏ Clear-coat ❏ Conventional

Wheel Cleaner
- ❏ All-purpose
- ❏ Chrome & wire wheel
- ❏ Polished or anodized aluminum
- ❏ Bare aluminum or magnesium

Tire Detailing Products
- ❏ Tire cleaner
- ❏ Rubber & vinyl protectant

Wheel & Trim Polish
- ❏ Chrome and metal polish
- ❏ Plastic polish

Interior & Vinyl-top Detailing Products
- ❏ Upholstery/top shampoo
    - ❏ Fabric ❏ Vinyl
- ❏ Carpet shampoo
- ❏ Leather cleaner
- ❏ Leather conditioner

Additional Detailing Products
- ❏ Engine degreaser
- ❏ Engine touch-up paint
- ❏ Accessory and chassis touch-up paint

Detailing Tools
- ❏ Wax applicator pad
- ❏ Toothbrush, detail brushes
- ❏ Scrub brushes
- ❏ Swabs
- ❏ Terry cloth towels (6 minimum)
- ❏ Clean T-shirt rags
- ❏ Window towels (lint-free cotton)
- ❏ Small dust pan and whisk broom
- ❏ Household vacuum cleaner
- ❏ Liquid applicator

Optional:
- ❏ Electric orbital buffer
- ❏ Spare bonnets

do-it-right